Walking with Jesus
the Path of Discipleship

Bruce Goettsche and Rick Goettsche

Table of Contents

Preface

This is the second book on which we have collaborated. Our first book together (*Difficult People: Dealing with Those Who Drive You Crazy*) was written while Rick was a senior in college.

Since that time we united as a pastoral team at the Union Church of La Harpe Illinois. Rick joined the pastoral staff in 2006. It has been a relationship we have enjoyed more than we ever hoped we would. We have been through some hard times. We have taken turns holding each other up, providing strength when it was lacking in the other person. We are Father and Son but we are also friends and partners in ministry.

We love what we do. It is a calling that fills us with a sense of humble joy. What a privilege to serve the King of Kings every day! It is not what most people think of as a job.

Every sermon we prepare is, in a sense, a collaboration. When one of us prepares to preach, the sermon is first read by the other person. We freely make comments that are always received gratefully. We have edited this as a whole volume and not as individual parts. Our passion is singular: we want to present the truth of Scripture in a way that is accurate, understandable, and practical. It is our practice to preach systematically through a book of the Bible.

We believe the Bible is the inspired, infallible, Word of God. Because of this, we want to listen to what the text says rather than try to read into the text what we would *like* to say. We believe the Bible speaks with superior (and essential) wisdom. We hope you will find that we have done this faithfully and effectively.

At the end of each chapter you will find questions. We hope you use these for personal review or for group study. We would love to see small groups using this book as a guide in their own study.

Throughout the book we will use the first person except when it is important for you to know which of us is making the comment.

Bruce and Rick Goettsche (2019)

Bruce and Rick Goettsche

Introduction

What does it mean to live like a follower of Jesus? You can find as many answers to this question as there are people. In this book we look at the answer the Apostle Paul gives to the question by looking at his practical instruction in the book of Ephesians.

We feel this is an important question to address at this time because the word "Christian" is used loosely to describe all kinds of people.

- People holding up hate signs at military funerals, football games, and any number of places because of a same sex attracted individual involved.
- Those who castigate various political figures.
- People who do not believe in the literal resurrection of Jesus or any of the miraculous elements of faith.
- White supremacists armed and ready for battle.
- Those who live indulgent lives and say they are doing so because God wants them to be blessed and they have simply claimed the blessing.
- Those who go to church on rare occasions and who seldom give any thought to Christ while conducting their normal lives, but tell everyone they are a Christian.
- Those who have strict codes of conduct related to attire, worship, and other areas of life and consider themselves believers because of this code.

We know you could add to this list but hopefully the point has been made: the term "Christian" is often used in ways that contradict the Biblical picture of a follower of Christ.

Paul focused less on externals and more on internals as he described the Christian life. This is because it is the Spirit-led life.

We focus in this book on the last three chapters (four through six) of Ephesians. The first three theologically rich chapters of Ephesians deserve volumes of their own. Many wonderful books have been written on the foundational theology you find in Ephesians 1-3 (D. Martyn

3

Lloyd-Jones has written many volumes on these chapters). The same is true for the armor of God in Ephesians 6. Consequently, we only briefly reference the armor of God. This illustration is also worthy of a book of its own (and many such books have been written. The masterpiece by William Gurnall is unequalled).

However, before moving on to the ethical teachings of Ephesians we do need to understand the first three chapters of the letter. It is accurate to say: you *cannot* rightly understand the ethical teachings without understanding the theology Paul lays down as a foundation. If you discount what is said in chapters 1-3 you will end up trying to be a Christian by being good! This is the opposite of what Paul is teaching!

Allow us to summarize. In the first three chapters the apostle Paul asserts several truths that are foundational to Christianity.

Salvation is God's idea and comes about by God's work.

Even before he made the world, God loved us and chose us in Christ to be holy and without fault in his eyes. God decided in advance to adopt us into his own family by bringing us to himself through Jesus Christ. This is what he wanted to do, and it gave him great pleasure. (Ephesians 1:4-5, NLT)

Rather than get bogged down in a discussion of predestination and election (which is fruitful, but beyond the scope of this book), see the big picture. It was God's plan all along to make us a part of His family through Christ. He is the initiator! He chose us. He awakened us. And He brought us to faith. God has a plan for our lives, and to live life fully we need to know His plan and depend on Him to fulfill it.

We used to be mired in sin but God made us alive!

Once you were dead because of your disobedience and your many sins. You used to live in sin, just like the rest of the world, obeying the devil—the commander of the powers in the unseen world. He is the spirit at work in the hearts of those who refuse to obey God. All of us used to live that way, following

4

the passionate desires and inclinations of our sinful nature. By our very nature we were subject to God's anger, just like everyone else.

But God is so rich in mercy, and he loved us so much, that even though we were dead because of our sins, he gave us life when he raised Christ from the dead. (Ephesians 2:1-5, NLT)

Understanding the depth of our addiction to sin is the key to understanding the magnitude and expansive beauty of grace. Paul said we were DEAD in our trespasses and our sin. We were not merely sick or wounded. We were spiritually dead and unable to respond to God.

For the purpose of our discussion of "What is a Christian?" we must note that GOD made us alive. In other words, a Christian is a person who has experienced a supernatural work of God. This person is awakened by God's Spirit and then filled with the same Spirit who teaches us how to live the life we were created to live.

Please get this: we do not make ourselves alive! You can work as hard as you want and try to be as "good" as you can muster, but you cannot make yourself right with God. You cannot EVER earn Heaven!

From time to time we talk to people who are dying. We routinely ask them if they are ready to meet the Lord. The majority of the time people respond by saying, "I think I have lived a pretty good life. Hopefully, it has been good enough." To this statement we routinely respond, "I can assure you, it has not been good enough!" Generally, with that answer, we have the person's attention.

We are not made right with God because we are good. We are made right with God because Christ was good and He gave His life for our sin!

The true believer is the person who has come to the end of themselves. They have given up trying to earn Heaven and have come running to Jesus for salvation.

The true believer understands that Christ alone provides the full payment for our sin. He alone can rescue us. His resurrection shows that the sacrifice of Christ was sufficient for our sin. It is possible, through Christ, to stand before God as if we had never sinned!!

Because of this salvation we now have an inheritance from God.

There are wonderful benefits of being God's child.

> *And when you believed in Christ, he identified you as his own by giving you the Holy Spirit, whom he promised long ago. The Spirit is God's guarantee that he will give us the inheritance he promised and that he has purchased us to be his own people. He did this so we would praise and glorify him. (Ephesians 1:13-14, NLT)*

God not only declared us (like a Judge), to be not-guilty because of what Jesus did on our behalf, He also took up residence inside of us to help us learn to live as children of the King!

The ethical and moral commands given by the Apostle Paul in the pages ahead **cannot be obeyed apart from the power of God's Spirit working in us!** These words are not a prescription for how to make yourself right with God; they are a description of what a person who is truly right with God looks like in practice. (Read that last sentence again…it is important!)

Paul continued to declare **this is the way of salvation for everyone, Jew and Gentile.** There is only one way for anyone to be made right with God…through Christ!

A true believer is not identified by what he or she is against or the cause they champion. They are known by their humble heart; a result of knowing they are made right with God not because of what they have done, but through the work of Christ on their behalf.

As Paul thinks about these great truths he says,

> *I pray that from his glorious, unlimited resources he will empower you with inner strength through his Spirit. Then Christ will make his home in your hearts as you trust in him. Your roots will grow down into God's love and keep you strong. And may you have the power to understand, as all God's people should,*

how wide, how long, how high, and how deep his love is. May you experience the love of Christ, though it is too great to understand fully. Then you will be made complete with all the fullness of life and power that comes from God.

Now all glory to God, who is able, through his mighty power at work within us, to accomplish infinitely more than we might ask or think. Glory to him in the church and in Christ Jesus through all generations forever and ever! Amen. (Ephesians 3:16-21, NLT)

The starting point for living out the life of the Spirit is a heart that is humbled by grace and motivated by love. It is a heart softened by mercy rather than hardened by arrogance. It is a heart that yearns to point to Jesus rather than exalt self.

If you understand the first part of Ephesians (in other words, if you understand the heart of the gospel) and have embraced it with all you are, then you are ready for the guidance of Ephesians 4:1-6:4.

We will look at the ethical commands of the Apostle Paul and try to understand and apply these commands while continually returning to the truth that we are made new by the grace of God through Christ. We will be intensely practical while at the same time continuously reminding you that the work that must be done can only be done in the power of the Spirit.

Dig Deeper

1. What is the significance of the fact that we were DEAD in sin?
2. How would you define "grace" (Ephesians 2:8)?
3. Why does someone have to be made right with God through Christ before they can follow the commands in the second half of the letter?
4. Do you believe it is true that no one has lived a good enough life to get into Heaven? Why or why not? How do you think the average person would answer this question?

Bruce and Rick Goettsche

1
Living in Balance
Ephesians 4:1-3

I am not an "auto guy" but even I can tell when my tires are severely out of balance. The car and even the steering wheel start to shake. Balanced tires are necessary for your car to run smoothly. In much the same way we need balance in our lives to live effectively.

As you read Paul's letters one of the things you will marvel at is his balance. He helps us understand what is true by teaching doctrine clearly and effectively. However, he doesn't leave us with notebooks of information. He turns his attention to the practical aspects of how this doctrine should impact the way we live. Belief and practice must be in balance.

The unbalanced believer is either: frequently arguing over some theological construct, or they go to the other extreme and say, "I don't believe in doctrine" (which of course is a doctrinal assertion!) They say the only thing that matters is what "works." That attitude opens us up to all kinds of false teaching. We can easily conclude something works because it results in what we want. That leaves "truth" open to individual interpretation. "Truth" that changes with the individual isn't really truth at all. It is opinion. We are searching for truth.

Let's tune in as Paul begins to apply the solid doctrine of Ephesians 1-3 to daily living.

> *As a prisoner for the Lord, then, I urge you to live a life worthy of the calling you have received. Be completely humble and gentle; be patient, bearing with one another in love. Make every effort to keep the unity of the Spirit through the bond of peace. (Ephesians 4:1-3)*

Live Lives that Are Worthy

Paul lays out an overarching principle: we should live in a way that befits the calling we have received. Let me stop here and remind you that Paul is NOT saying we should live lives that will be worthy (or deserving) of salvation. We will never earn salvation! He says we should live as those who have been granted forgiveness and new life even though we do not deserve it.

The word "worthy" in the Greek is the word *AXIOS* which is the word from which we derive the word axiom or axiomatic. An axiom is a self-evident truth. Paul is saying we should live lives that are right, appropriate, and even obvious for someone who is called a child of God.

When Kate Middleton and Prince William were considering marriage, I am sure that Ms. Middleton was talked to about the responsibility of living a life of royalty. Every "royal" knows that there is a certain standard of behavior that is required of their position.

It is the same with someone who serves as an Ambassador or even one who serves in the military. These people are reminded that they represent the United States and should live in a way that brings honor to their country. We see the same thing with teachers, pastors and other public officials...position often dictates behavior.

Paul argues that since we are now children of God, we should live in a way that shows others that we have been made new in Christ. People should see the influence of God's resident Spirit reflected in us by the way we live. Lest we misunderstand, Paul gets specific.

Adopt the Right Attitude

External behavior is determined by our internal disposition. Because of this Paul writes, "Be completely humble and gentle; be patient, bearing with one another in love." He gives us four attitudes or characteristics that should be evidenced in our lives.

The first attitude is humility. In the world, humility is often viewed as a negative. Some see it as an indicator of low self-esteem. Christians however, view it differently. Christ told us that God esteems the one who is humble. Jesus is our model of humility.

This is a difficult concept in a society that is constantly telling us to "sell ourselves" and to "look out for number 1" (which sounds a great deal like exhorting us to be selfish). We are taught to not let anyone "take advantage of us." Tim Keller has written an excellent little 48-page booklet on humility titled, "The Freedom of Self-forgetfulness." He makes a keen observation,

> Up until the twentieth century, traditional cultures (and this is still true of most cultures in the world) always believed that too high a view of yourself was the root cause of all the evil in the world. What is the reason for most of the crime and violence in the world? Why are people abused? Why are people cruel? Why do people do the bad things they do? Traditionally, the answer was hubris – the Greek word meaning pride or too high a view of yourself. Traditionally, that was the reason given for why people misbehave.
>
> But, in our modern western culture, we have developed an utterly opposite cultural consensus. The basis of contemporary education, the way we treat incarcerated prisoners, the foundation of most modern legislation and the starting point for modern counseling is exactly the opposite of the traditional consensus. Our belief today – and it is deeply rooted in everything – is that people misbehave for lack of self-esteem and because they have too low a view of themselves.[1]

So what is humility? Humility is seeing ourselves as redeemed people. The humble person knows that they cannot earn God's favor. They stand by grace alone. We are not the center of the universe and therefore everything should not be evaluated by how it affects us.

C.S. Lewis in his masterpiece, "Mere Christianity" wrote,

> If we were to meet a truly humble person, Lewis says, we would never come away from meeting them thinking they were humble...the thing we would remember from meeting a truly gospel-humble person is how much they seemed to

be totally interested in us. Because the essence of gospel-humility is not thinking more of myself or thinking less of myself, it is thinking of myself less."[2]

A humble person therefore is one who no longer feels that it is "all about me." They serve the Lord, not themselves. Since they are not spending all their time thinking about what they desire, they have the ability to consider the needs and feelings of others. Because they do not see everything from a selfish perspective they are more pliable to the influence of God's Spirit.

The second character trait or attitude is that of **"meekness" or "gentleness."** Again, our society (at least American society) equates meekness with weakness. We think of a meek person as a 90-pound weakling who spends his life just trying to stay out of everyone else's way. That is not what this word means! It is not about weakness, it is actually about *strength under control.*

Aristotle saw the term as the mid-point between being too angry and never being angry at all. The meek person is angry at the wrongs and suffering of others but does not get angry when he himself is insulted and treated wrongly.

Maybe it would help to see the opposite of this meekness or gentleness. A person who lacks meekness or gentleness

- Takes offense quickly
- Will constantly correct you (demonstrating their superiority)
- Will blast away at you and excuse it saying, "I'm only being honest"
- Will constantly remind you of your failures
- Will be apathetic (they don't care)

A person who has experienced the wonder of God's underserved and unfathomable grace seeks to extend that same kind of grace to those around them. They should be soft rather than harsh; loving rather than combative.

Third, we are told we should have an attitude characterized by **"patience" or "long-suffering."** Since God has shown such patience to us, we should reflect that patience in our dealing with others. Patience means: to endure with another.

If you have a family pet and a little child you have probably observed patience in the pet. The child may squeeze and hang on the animal and the animal endures it (at least for a while). They know instinctively that the child (though annoying) is merely showing love.

Patience is not weakness or even inaction; it is living your life under control. The patient person is the one who doesn't give up. They focus on the big picture. They see beyond the present circumstances. They know real change takes time.

Think about a patient teacher. A patient teacher is the one that doesn't get discouraged because a child doesn't understand something immediately. They don't conclude that the child is a "lost cause." The patient teacher understands that different people learn best in different ways. They continue to try different things in the belief that once they find a way to connect or reach the child, that child can learn as well as any.

A patient coach is one who doesn't give all his time to the naturally gifted athletes. He continues to instruct and work with the lesser players because he knows and believes three things: 1) Talented players will not excel unless those who are around them do their job. 2) Some of the most successful players were people who did not start with natural ability. 3) Coaching is not just about winning games (unless you are a pro), it is about instilling character and discipline in the athletes.

The patient believer sees other people not in terms of their failures, but in terms of their potential in Christ.

The **fourth attitude or character trait is love**. The word used here is the word "agape." As you probably know, the Greek language had four different words for love. The first three referred to: intimacy, friendship, and familial love. Agape is a unique Christian kind of love. It is the kind of love that God shows to us. William Barclay says,

> *The real meaning of agapē is unconquerable benevolence. If we regard a person with agapē, it means that nothing that he can do will make us seek anything but his highest good. Though he injure us and insult us, we will never feel anything but kindness towards him. That quite clearly means that this Christian love is not an emotional thing.*

This agapē is a thing, not only of the emotions, but also of the will.[3]

This is the kind of love God has for us and wants us to extend to others. This kind of love is uncommon and can only be produced by the work of the Spirit in the human heart. It is unnatural just like all the other traits. When we act in these ways we show that we are not controlled by the flesh but by the Spirit.

The finest definition of the love God wants us to show to each other is found in 1 Corinthians 13,

> *Love is patient, love is kind. It does not envy, it does not boast, it is not proud. It is not rude, it is not self-seeking, it is not easily angered, it keeps no record of wrongs. Love does not delight in evil but rejoices with the truth. It always protects, always trusts, always hopes, always perseveres. (1 Corinthians 13:4-7)*

Paul tells us to be *completely* controlled by these four traits. They should be the traits that characterize our life rather than things that show up in rare glimpses of godliness.

Paul gives us a directive which would indicate that we need to cultivate and develop these traits in our lives. How do we do this? Let me give you some suggestions:

The first step, which may surprise you, is to **study doctrine**. As we come to understand the nature of sin, the concept of grace, and the character of God, we start to see ourselves differently. We understand that we are recipients of an undeserved grace. We see that our salvation is not dependent on us being "better" than others, but is wholly anchored to the love of God in Christ. That fact alone will make us more humble.

Second, we need to **spend much time with God**. It is a demonstrable fact that we become like those with whom we spend the most time. The influence is inevitable. If we spend most of our time allowing the secular world to feed us their values through television, movies, music, and news shows, we will adopt the attitudes of those people. If, on the other hand, we give significant time to the things of God and to God's community of people, we will be influenced more by those values and attitudes. Read the Bible and read other Christian books. Listen to Christian music. Make time to be quiet before the Lord. But above all, spend time with the Lord Himself!

Third, we need to *actively cultivate these traits in our lives.* Learn about the traits, pray about their growth in your life, daily take a good hard look at your encounters with others, and listen to the counsel of significant mentors and friends. Find some people who know they have your permission and are encouraged to hold you accountable.

All of these traits are somewhat "counter-cultural." They will take time and effort to develop. However, by God's grace we can move in the right direction.

The Goal We Pursue

Paul says, we have a specific goal in developing these traits.

> *Make every effort to keep the unity of the Spirit*
> *through the bond of peace. (Ephesians 4:3)*

Have you noticed that everyone around you seems to be on edge? It is almost like they are looking for a fight. Any little offense and they will blow up or attack. Any perceived slight and they will walk away and conclude that your relationship with them is over. We have experienced this from people many times.

As we mentioned, we wrote a book a number of years ago titled, *Difficult People: Dealing with Those Who Drive You Crazy.* The book had a pretty simple premise: most conflict could be ended if we simply changed *our* attitude. If we made *some* effort at pursuing peace, forgiveness, and reconciliation, most problems would disappear. If we were willing to "rather be wronged" than to take offense and fight, we would preserve the unity of the Spirit and the bond of peace.

Paul does not tell us to create unity; he encourages us to *keep* the unity. The Holy Spirit produces unity. We are unified by the work of God on our behalf through Christ. In other words, we have unity with other believers until we destroy it. We do this by our

- Competition rather than cooperation with each other.
- Selfishness (insisting on our preferences).
- Quibbling over secondary issues.

15

- Focus on advancing our "church" over the Kingdom of God.
- Impatience...we give up on others much too easily.

Our job is to maintain unity rather than dismantle it.

Unity must never come at the expense of doctrine! This is that balance issue again. There are some who say "doctrine divides." The Bible however tells us just the opposite: it is doctrine that makes us one! It is our common experience of God's grace extended to us through Christ's sacrificial death and powerful resurrection that make us one. Without doctrine, we cannot have true unity in the Spirit!

When Jesus prayed in the Garden, His prayer was that we (his followers) might be "one even as He and the father are one." Unity in the church fosters growth. Unity enables us to influence society with one strong voice rather than many voices that are cancelling each other out. Unity among God's diverse people is a wonderful testimony to a fractured world.

We must carefully weigh what are *essential* doctrines and what are secondary doctrines; essential doctrines are those that are explicitly taught in the Bible. We can disagree on the unclear issues (such as the timetable of the end-times, the application of the rite of baptism, the frequency of communion, the structure of church government) and still move forward as brothers and sisters in Christ.

Conclusion

Let's do a little personal evaluation. Stop and ask yourself a simple question: What should a true child of God look like? How should they treat other people? How should they behave in a time of conflict? How should they treat someone who has failed or fallen? There is a good chance that you already have a sense of what it really means to walk in a manner worthy of the gospel. To a large degree it is self-evident or axiomatic.

So here is the question: Are you living the way you know you should as a child of God? If not, what needs to change? Is your doctrine faulty? Are there attitudes you need to cultivate?

God has called us to be His ambassadors in the world. We represent Him to those around us. Let's represent Him well!

Dig Deeper

1. Why is right doctrine a prerequisite to living as a believer in a lost world?
2. How do the Biblical definitions of humility and meekness differ from the definitions of the world around us?
3. Try to write 1 Corinthians 13 using descriptions that would describe the popular culture's definition of love.
4. If you are in a situation where you can't be in agreement doctrinally, can you have unity? What questions should be asked?
5. Which of these characteristics do you think is the most difficult and why? (Humility, meekness and gentleness, patience and love)

Bruce and Rick Goettsche

.

2
One Body
Ephesians 4:4-13

One of the biggest (and justifiable) criticisms of the church is related to the factions within Christianity. In the United States alone there are better than 2000 different denominations! There are so many different kinds of churches that people are understandably confused. Churches compete with each other like businesses trying to hold on to their "market share." This is not God's design.

In the high priestly prayer of Jesus in John 17, He twice prayed that we might be one, just as He and the Father are one (verses 21 and 23). He prayed our unity would be a testimony to the world that Christ was truly sent by God. Unity in the body of Christ is supposed to be a hallmark of the new community of saints.

We have already seen this theme several times in Ephesians. Paul told us Jews and Gentiles, who used to view each other as enemies, are now, through Christ, brothers and sisters. He told us that we are to make every effort to preserve our unity. Paul emphasized this subject so we can draw a couple of conclusions right away. **First, the issue of unity must be important.** When a particular theme is returned to repeatedly we should take note. It is emphasized because it is something God wants to make sure we don't miss.

Second, Paul's emphasis may reveal that unity was a problem in the early church. Knocking down barriers that had existed for many years was not easy. The church consisted of rich and poor, slave and free, Jew and Gentile, men and women. All of these barriers needed to come down to have true unity in the church. We could learn from their experiences. Listen to Paul's words.

> *There is one body and one Spirit— just as you were called to one hope when you were called— one Lord, one faith, one baptism; one God and Father of all, who is over all and through all and in all. (Ephesians 4:4-6)*

The Unity of the Church

In these short three verses the apostle Paul used the word "one" seven different times! He said God is the Father "of all, over all, through all and in all." Here is that repetition for emphasis thing again.

Paul is making some simple yet important points when it comes to unity. **There is only One God.** Paul wants us to see the absurdity of a divisive spirit. There is only one Father, One Son, One Holy Spirit. There is only one way of salvation and only one hope of eternal life.

Admittedly, we wince just a little when Paul mentions one "baptism." Baptism is one of the most divisive issues in the church. We divide over the meaning of baptism (is it necessary for salvation, or does it testify to salvation?); we divide over who should be baptized (believers only, or adult believers and the children of believers); and we divide over the amount of water that is necessary for baptism.

In 1 Corinthians 12:13 Paul wrote,

> *For we were all baptized by one Spirit into one body – whether Jews or Greeks, slave or free – and we were all given the one Spirit to drink.*

Paul is not talking about the mechanics of baptism. He is telling us that the act of Christian baptism (no matter how it is administered) is a declaration that we belong to the one true Lord. Baptism testifies that we have turned to the One who died in our place for forgiveness. It is an act of surrender to Him and as a result we claim the Holy Spirit as our seal and deposit.

Our unity is designed to reveal God's own character. God is One. Even though many people worship different gods, that does not mean there *are* numerous gods. No matter what your "belief system," there is only one true God! We are not given license to create God in our image. We are created in HIS image!

Eugene Peterson captures Paul's message with freshness in The Message,

> *You were all called to travel on the same road and in the same direction, so stay together, both outwardly and inwardly. You have one Master, one faith, one baptism, one*

God and Father of all, who rules over all, works through all, and is present in all. Everything you are and think and do is permeated with Oneness.

The point is clear: as God's people, we should reflect God's nature. He is One so we should be one. Unfortunately, the church is more often identified by division rather than oneness. So what is the problem?

Where Has Our Oneness Gone?

Our lack of unity can be traced to several issues. First, in some cases **unity has been lost because the faith has been compromised**. D. Martyn Lloyd-Jones wrote,

The tragedy is that men are trying to produce unity by telling us that it does not matter very much what we believe, that as long as we all come together and work together, and do not argue about doctrine, we shall all be one. But the unity of the Spirit comes through understanding, not through discounting understanding and saying that the knowledge of doctrine does not matter. The great characteristic of revival (where unity was strongest) is that men understand the doctrine and the truth in a way they have never done before. Not only so, they begin to rejoice as they have never done before, and are filled with an assurance and a sense of certainty of their relationship to God.[4]

Theologians make a distinction between the church visible and invisible. The visible church is made up of those who attend services or are members of churches. Not all of these people are genuine believers. People come to the church for a variety of reasons: for fellowship, out of habit, to appease someone, or out of a desire to be a "better person." Not all who attend church are Christ-followers.

The invisible church is the true "body of Christ." These are people who have all come to a point where they rely on Christ alone for their salvation. These people are in buildings and homes around the world with a variety of names on them. They have asked Christ to lead their lives and refashion their hearts. These people are the ones called to be one body in the One Father, Son, Holy Spirit, Faith, Hope, and baptism. However, even among genuine believers there is often division.

There is a second problem. We are divided because **we have yet to overcome the battle with our sinful nature and the self-centeredness that has dominated our lives**. As sinful human beings we tend to view every issue as a battleground where there has to be a winner and a loser. When there is some kind of disagreement we immediately make it a personal battle with a clear cut battle line. If you are right, then I am wrong. We don't like to be wrong.

We have a hard time accepting the fact that different sometimes just means "different." It doesn't mean "better than" or "worse than." It just means different. We must accept the fact that we might both be seeing only part of the story. The truth is always richer and deeper than what we perceive. Sometimes, we argue about trinkets at the expense of finding true treasure.

Men and women are different, they see things differently. This can create conflict or it can be part of the richness in marriage. Differences enrich when we reach the understanding that sometimes it is not about right and wrong. Sometimes we just see things differently.

As Christians we divide over methods, music, and management issues. We divide over the best translation of the Bible, the administration of baptism, the frequency of communion, and our experience with the Holy Spirit. We make preferences and personal conviction more important than the unity we are commanded to make "every effort" to preserve. All these issues are worth discussing. They are not worth division.

There is a third reason we lack unity. Unity is difficult because **we confuse unity with uniformity**. In other words, we mistakenly think that in order to be unified we have to have the same experience, preferences, and passions. That is the error Paul addresses next.

Unified Diversity

But to each one of us grace has been given as Christ apportioned it. This is why it says:

"When he ascended on high, he led captives in his train and gave gifts to men."

(What does "he ascended" mean except that he also descended to the lower, earthly regions? He who descended is the very one who ascended higher than all the heavens, in order to fill the whole universe.) It was he who gave some to be apostles, some to be prophets, some to be evangelists, and some to be pastors and teachers, to prepare God's people for works of service, so that the body of Christ may be built up until we all reach unity in the faith and in the knowledge of the Son of God and become mature, attaining to the whole measure of the fullness of Christ. (Ephesians 4:7-13)

Paul appealed to Psalm 68:18 to underscore his contention that everyone in the body of Christ has a job to do. He argued that the passage, which alludes to the practice of victorious kings coming back from battle, is a picture of Jesus. Jesus came down from Heaven, gained victory, and upon His return to Heaven, gave gifts to His soldiers.

Paul teaches us that the church is unified yet diverse in its expression of oneness. We are one in heart and spirit yet serve the Lord in different ways. Paul teaches about this diversity (often called spiritual gifts) in many places. The most extensive passage is in 1 Corinthians 12. If we lay this passage alongside our text in Ephesians we get a fuller picture of what Paul is teaching.

God has given each of us (1 Cor. 12:7) an expression of His grace or a "spiritual gift." In other words He has given everyone a job to do. This is also called a "manifestation of the Spirit." When the Holy Spirit takes up residence in our lives He also equips us to serve God in a significant way.

No matter how many times we talk about spiritual gifts there are some who will say, "I don't have a spiritual gift." All I can say to that statement is: "If that is true, then you are not a believer." The Bible is clear: EACH ONE is given a manifestation of grace for the common good. Everyone has a job to do!

The confusion about gifts often comes from the idea that spiritual gifts must be public or dramatic. That is not the case. Think of a Broadway show. We see the performers on the stage. However, there is an entire army of gifted people we do not see: the script writers, musicians, the Director, set designers, people who work with props, ticket takers, publicity people, backup performers, agents and much much more. The body of Christ is like this. Just because you are not "on stage" does not mean you don't have a significant gift.

Sometimes your "gift" is something you are already doing. You look at your actions and believe you are "not doing anything special." But what you are doing may be something other people cannot do.

We'll discuss how you find your gift(s) shortly.

Second, these gifts are given at God's discretion (1 Corinthians 12:11). Our spiritual gift is not a prize we earn, or even a sign of our status. It is the place we have been assigned by God in accordance with His wisdom and will. I do not believe every spiritual gift is listed in the Bible. All the lists in the Bible differ so I think we are given samples of the kinds of gifts God gives. Since God gives gifts at His discretion, He can adapt the gifts to the changing needs of the church in a changing society.

Third, the purpose of the gifts is to build up the body. Spiritual gifts are designed to strengthen the unity and growth of the church. If the exercise of our gift causes division, we are not exercising the gift correctly. If our gift is causing others to stumble, it is not being used correctly. We are not given spiritual gifts to show off or to promote ourselves. Our gifts do not show who is more spiritual than the next guy. The gifts have one purpose: to build up and enrich the body of Christ.

Fourth, the church is meant to be interdependent. In 1 Corinthians 12:14-24 the apostle Paul points out that just like a body, the various parts need to work together. Every gift is important. Think about the effect on your body when a toenail is ripped off. A toenail may not be prominent, but no one can say it is insignificant. Most of our bodily organs are not seen, yet if they stop working we are in big trouble. If the cells in our body (which we can't see with the naked eye) don't do what they are supposed to do, we end up ill and perhaps die.

I learned this lesson the hard way once. I was having problem with my car early in my youth ministry days. I did some research (this was before the days of YouTube and Google) and determined that the "head gasket" needed to be replaced. Even though I knew I was in over my head (no pun intended) I took the valve cover off and replaced the gasket. However, as I put it all back together I couldn't get a couple of the bolts back in. I concluded, "These are probably unnecessary anyway." I tried to start the car but it wouldn't work. I tried everything (including kicking the car, I'm sure). The next day I called a mechanic friend to help me. I explained the situation. When he stopped laughing, he asked for the bolts, put them in and explained that I was destroying the vacuum (or something) by leaving the bolts out. You may feel like an "extra bolt" but you are necessary!

God created us to be incomplete without each other. When a person tells you that you must have the same experience or gift as they have had, they reveal both enormous arrogance and a severe misunderstanding of what the Bible teaches.

Finally, Paul tells us that spiritual gifts are to be used in love (1 Corinthians 13) and that all the gifts should be used in a "fitting and orderly way" (1 Corinthians 14:40). Once again let's state: if the use of our gifts results in division or hurts another person, we are not using our gift correctly.

Find Your Place

In light of what we have seen, I hope you see that it is important to find your place. Many people feel frustrated because they can't identify (or label) their gift. Let me reiterate, just because you don't have a "prominent gift" (you can't speak in public, carry or play a tune, or disciple children) that doesn't mean you don't have a role to play. In fact, I think it takes a greater faithfulness to continue to do what you have been enabled to do…even when no one but God sees that faithfulness.

Some will ask: But what can I do to help me discover my spiritual gift? How do I find what it is that God has given me to do? Here are some simple guidelines:

Don't make this harder than you need to. Most of the things God has called us to do are right in front of us. God prepares our hearts, gives us the abilities, and provides the circumstances for us to serve Him effectively. Most likely your area of service is right in front of you. It may be something you are already doing.

Understand spiritual gifts by studying what is taught in the Bible. In addition to this passage, read the other passages about spiritual gifts carefully. Read through 1 Corinthians 12-14, and Romans 12:3-8. Follow the cross-references. Learn the purpose of the gifts.

Ask God to reveal to you how He wants you to serve Him. Be careful here! It is not a matter of telling God what you want to do...it is about asking Him to show you what He wants you to do.

Look at what it is that you are good at and what you have an interest in. There are times in the Bible when God has called people to jobs they did not want (think about Moses and some of the prophets). However the notion that serving God means doing something distasteful or way beyond our skill set is in error. God equips us for our jobs with the skills, and I believe, the passions or desires, to serve as He directs. In other words, look at what you are *already doing* or would like to do and find a way to do that to the glory of God. Look for a way you can use your talents and abilities to build up the body of Christ. We often conclude that because we are satisfied or enjoy doing something it cannot be from God. That is wrong thinking.

Listen to others. Sometimes we are blind to our own gifts. Pay attention to the things people see in you. By the same token, help others by pointing out the areas where you recognize expressions of God's grace in their lives.

Experiment. There may be things you have a desire to do or feel a "calling" to do but you don't know whether you have the skills. Experiment. Find out if you have those skills by volunteering. Go into the job with an open mind. Understand that some skills must be developed, give yourself time to learn. Remind yourself that you have not "failed" if you aren't good at something. If something doesn't work, it may mean it is not your gift, it may mean it is not the right setting, or it may mean it is not the right time. God honors those who step out in faith in an effort to discern His will. If we truly are open to His leading, we will be led.

Finally, *don't limit God.* He may be calling you to do something that is fresh and new. He may lead you to do something that has never been done before. Just because your interests are different doesn't mean they are wrong (unless of course, they are sinful).

Conclusion

If we have heard what the apostle is teaching, then we know there is work to do. Our challenge is to focus more on building bridges and finding points of agreement that lead to us working with other churches rather than enumerating weaknesses and competing with these other believers. We need to see other believers as part of our family rather than as our competition. Rather than pick at each other, we must make an effort to encourage each other.

I believe we not only CAN but we MUST stand together in the cause of Christ. A military force that is fighting each other will not, and cannot, win against a formidable enemy. Our enemy is the most formidable of all. If we do not stand together, we will fall separately. The Christian community has lost influence in our culture because we do not stand together. Our country's moral decline is partially because of a divided church. The unity of the church is important for our future.

We must also fight the notion and trend toward spectator Christianity. Too many believe that you pay someone (a Pastor) to do ministry. Your job is to hold that person accountable and to give money to their support. Paul says Pastors are supposed to help "equip the saints for ministry." The work God has called us to do requires "all hands on deck." If we want to be "healthy" we need all the parts of the body to be functioning.

Here are some suggestions for becoming a bridge-builder:

- Take an interest in other churches. Learn what they believe and why. Ask questions, not to fight…but to understand. Even if we don't agree with something, we can appreciate that people have Biblical reasons for what they are doing.
- Resolve to speak positively of your own church, Pastor and congregation AND the people and leaders of the other churches near you.
- Remind yourself constantly that different is not "better than" or "worse than," it is just different.

- Take advantage of ministries other churches are providing that you do not have. Don't let the "spirit of competition" keep you from growing in Christ.
- Pray for unity and understanding.

God has called us to something wonderful, and the only way we will be able to do it is by working together.

Dig Deeper

1. Have you ever been involved in a church conflict? If so, what was it about? What was the result?
2. Why does division and competition between churches confuse unbelievers and new believers? Why do you think there is so much division and competition?
3. What have you been taught about spiritual gifts?
4. What gift(s) do you think you might have? Why do you think so? (It is valuable to ask others what they perceive your gifts to be?)
5. What can you do to help other people find their spiritual gifts?

3
A Picture of Maturity
Ephesians 4:11-16

No one comes to faith in Christ as a mature believer. Our status with God changes the moment we believe, but our thinking and lifestyle change over the course of our lifetime. The Bible (especially Paul) likes to refer to young or immature believers as infants in faith. It's a good analogy. We begin our faith limited in knowledge and ability. Paul points out some similarities immature believers have with children, then contrasts that with the goal of maturity. The remainder of the book of Ephesians will expand this discussion of what it means to live as mature followers of Christ.

> *It was he who gave some to be apostles, some to be prophets, some to be evangelists, and some to be pastors and teachers, to prepare God's people for works of service, so that the body of Christ may be built up until we all reach unity in the faith and in the knowledge of the Son of God and become mature, attaining to the whole measure of the fullness of Christ. Then we will no longer be infants, tossed back and forth by the waves, and blown here and there by every wind of teaching and by the cunning and craftiness of men in their deceitful scheming. Instead, speaking the truth in love, we will in all things grow up into him who is the Head, that is, Christ. From him the whole body, joined and held together by every supporting ligament, grows and builds itself up in love, as each part does its work. (Ephesians 4:11-16)*

In the last chapter we learned every believer has a place where God wants us to "plug in." Like the human body, the church is considered healthy when all its parts are working together, and considered sick when one or more parts are not working; Our goal is to become healthy and mature. In order to help us understand the concept, Paul draws a picture of what this maturity looks like. He shows us what maturity is NOT and then what it IS by contrast.

What Maturity is Not

Fickleness. Children are "tossed back and forth by the waves." This is easy to observe. One day (or in some cases, one moment) children are the best of friends, the next they appear to be mortal enemies. One day they are privy to the secrets of others that are being shared, the next day they are the ones who are having their secrets exposed.

Children are like little chameleons. They adopt the characteristics of their environment. When they are with one group of people they like what that group likes and when they are with another group, they like what that group likes. Children are not concerned about truth and error; they are concerned about being liked. We tell our kids that it doesn't matter if the other kids like them. This only leads our children to conclude that we are hopelessly out of touch.

Children are constantly changing their interests. A little baby will stare at you and even engage with you for a long time. You may feel that you have really "connected." However, suddenly you will be forgotten and their attention will be focused on something or someone else that is more "amusing" (like a light or ceiling fan).

An immature believer is like this. Their theology (or belief system) is determined by whichever speaker they listened to or whatever conference they attended most recently. They are undiscerning. They have not learned to weigh and examine what they hear, they lack a solid foundation. These people are your friends one moment and critically tearing you apart in the next. They jump from church to church always picking fault and telling you they need to be in a place where the people or Pastor are "more faithful to the truth" or something along that line. These people create instability.

Gullibility. Why do little children fall for the "I've got your nose" trick? Why is it so easy to convince them that you have pulled a quarter out of their ear? It is because they are gullible! If you talk about monsters convincingly they will believe monsters exist and won't be able to sleep.

This is why you need to monitor what your children watch on television. They have a hard time distinguishing between truth and error; real and pretend.

I had an experience at our AWANA youth program (our group goes from children 3 years old through 5th grade). One of the children was very concerned and confessed to me, "I lost my Awana book." My immediate response was to give them a hard time by saying, "Well, I guess we will have to string you up and hang you from your feet!" Tears welled up in her eyes. I quickly told her I was kidding and that she did not need to worry because our Awana Secretary kept really good records and we would get her another book. I was reminded that children take you seriously and literally even when you aren't being serious!

Gullibility is not confined to youth. We know that in a political campaign the success of the campaign hangs on how the campaign can spin the news reports and revelations that come out. It is about getting people to believe certain truths about you and your opponent. That is why they never really answer the questions in a debate. They are concerned about getting "their message" out.

Scam artists are skilled at getting people to believe they have won great sums of money and all that is needed is for you to give them an account number so they can deposit the funds in your account. I had a time when someone called and told me I had won a free trip to Jamaica for two. I decided to play along.

I asked the caller how much this trip was going to cost me. He said it would cost me nothing. I told him he should send me the tickets and reservations. He said he wanted to tell me about a great deal first. He hemmed and hawed and we did a little verbal dance. It turned out that the free trip was only if I purchased some vitamins and went on the automatic renewal program. I pointed out that the trip was not free. He argued that it was. He ended the conversation frustrated and I was amused. (I never received my tickets to Jamaica).

Immature believers are susceptible to those who are deceptive and manipulative in their teaching. The false teachers have several tactics,

- Their most popular tactic is to misquote the Bible. They will quote a passage like "Judge not, lest you be judged" and say that it means it is wrong to make moral judgments. However, if you read further in the text Jesus tells us to make more judgments!

31

The command about judging is about our attitude (adopting a superior and judgmental attitude) rather than about discerning and making judgments. You can prove anything from the Bible as long as you don't pay attention to the context.

- They will claim something is in the Bible that isn't really there. Have you ever heard someone say, "The Bible says, the Lord helps those who help themselves." That's not in the Bible! That is a quote from Ben Franklin! Or how about "the Lord will never give you more than you can handle? (Not in the Bible! The Lord often gives us more than we can handle so we are forced to trust Him!)
- These teachers will strengthen their point by quoting respected "experts" (often people you have never heard of). Or they will ridicule you saying, "No one believes that..." or "only the uneducated would think that way" (that is not an argument).

The only way to avoid being blown about by the winds of religious fads is to mature in your faith by anchoring yourself to the truth. We need to know and understand the Word of God. We learn discernment by knowing what God has taught and testing everything against that standard.

What Maturity Is

But what is it we are striving for? What are the characteristics of a mature follower of Christ? Paul lists several characteristics.

They use their spiritual gifts for God's glory. Remember the context of our passage? Paul has been arguing that the mature person is the One who is doing what God has called them to do. The mature believer knows God has called them to take an active part in the family of God. They have found (or are looking for) the contribution they can make and are serving in a way that brings honor to Him and health to the community of faith. For more information, review the last chapter.

They speak the truth in love. In other words, they speak, live, and do the truth. We should be truth-tellers because God is true. We should reflect His character.

Being a truth-teller is especially applicable when sharing the truth of the gospel. The gospel is the good news that God will make us new through Christ. Part of this truth is bad and hard to hear (that we are sinful and cannot *ever* save ourselves). However, people must understand the bad news about their sin before they can hear and appreciate the good news about forgiveness and new life through the sacrifice of Christ.

Immature people tend to embrace two opposite errors. The first error is speaking truth, but without love. They "blast away" at people without any semblance of compassion. They seem almost delighted to point out faults and failings. Sometimes they say, "I'm only telling you the truth because I love you." But you certainly don't feel any love in the words spoken.

The second error is to withhold the truth because you feel it is the loving thing to do. But most of the time we are not really withholding the words because it is loving; we are doing it because it is EASIER! We don't want conflict or hurt feelings, so we withhold truth. However, if you see someone doing something destructive, and you don't say something, is that really loving? Of course not! The loving person acts with the best interest of the person at heart. They would rather risk a "difficult conversation" if that is what is needed.

You can see these extremes in some families. On one extreme is the parent who is always criticizing their child. They are harsh and if you look closely you can see the spirit of the child draining. This parent lacks love. On the other hand you see parents who never discipline their child. They say they want their child to feel loved and supported. The truth however is that the parent wants to be liked. We want to say to such parents: "You are supposed to be the parent and at times, when you are doing what parents are supposed to do, your children aren't going to like you. Your job is not to be their friend, but to help them grow and mature!"

Truth telling is about balance. We are to speak the uncompromising truth with compassion and love. When Jesus sent out the disciples, He said: "be as wise as serpents, and as harmless as doves." (Matthew 10:16) This is the balance you will find in a mature believer.

There is one more factor here. We who desire to speak the truth in love must also be willing to receive loving truth from others. Rather than immediately becoming defensive, we must ask if we need to hear what is being spoken. We need to let people help us grow. That leads to the last point.

They live an increasingly Christ-controlled life. You will frequently hear a child say, "Mine" or "It's my turn" or "Give it to me." Why? Because in a child's mind, the only thing that matters is what I want right now. The mature person is able to see beyond themselves. They see the impact of their choices on others. They are willing to surrender their will to the will of God.

You see this in believers and a church when

- A loving welcome is extended to all whether they are believers or not. Mature believers see potential rather than failures; beauty rather than scars.
- There is a resolute yet joyful love of the truth of God's Word. They are not interested in bending the Bible to support what they believe; they are interested in changing their lives to meet the truth revealed in the Word of God.
- There is a spirit of service. The mature person is no longer wrapped up in themselves. They now can see the heartache and needs of those around them. They are becoming more generous because they see their resources as gifts of God meant to serve others. They build up rather than tear down.
- There is a deep and heartfelt worship of the Lord because they see Him (rather than their desires) as the center of life. They see how small they really are and in contrast how big and wonderful God is.
- They have learned to listen with their eyes and with their hearts. They no longer approach conversations focused on "when will I be able to talk next" and instead are truly concerned about what another has to say.
- They are eager to learn. They want to learn from others but even more they want to spend time learning from the Lord of life. Consequently, prayer becomes less a chore and more like an audience with the most important person you know.
- They are not threatened by correction from others because they long to grow in maturity.

This is what the healthy and growing believer (and church) looks like. Mature people check their egos at the door. They know they are most fulfilled when they are most caught up in the person and work of Christ.

Conclusion

The question that remains is a practical one: "What do we need to do to travel the road to maturity in our faith?" As one who continues that process, let me comment on what I have observed so far.

First, we will grow in maturity only by spending time with the Lord. We will see where we suffer from immaturity most clearly by contrasting our lives with His standards and with His heart. Spending time with the One who is Holy will expose the problem areas of your life. It is not only important THAT we read the Word of God, it is also important HOW we read the Word of God.

We must hear God's Word like we would listen to the advice of a professional athlete about the sport we play. We need to listen to God's Word like we would listen to the keynote speaker at a conference on something we care about deeply. We listen as we would to our cherished mentor or closest friend. In other words, we do not listen to fulfill an obligation or assignment…we listen for guidance, and for information we need. We listen to the Bible's diagnosis of our problems because we know we are listening to the "specialist" on the soul. In other words, we should be tuned in. We must interact with what we are hearing.

It is the same with prayer. We do not talk with God as if it were a meeting with the principal at school; we talk with God as we would someone we love and care for. We long to connect, not simply talk. We cannot grow up into Christ until we truly get to know Christ!

Second, study those who appear to be more mature in the faith. A little child learns to walk and talk by mimicking others. They do what they see others doing (sometimes that's good and sometimes that's bad). In the same way, we will mature by following good models. So, look for someone who models the character of Christ. Look for someone who seems to be mature in faith. When you find someone like that, listen to them. Learn from them. Follow their example. Become their "apprentice" in the faith.

Brandon Marshall, a football player and excellent pass receiver said when he came to his first football camp he found the receiver that did what he wanted to be able to do and then did everything he did. He said he still studies the best receivers in football and tries to learn everything he can from them.

I have several people that I look up to. I read everything they write. When they speak, I listen. When they teach, I take notes. I watch what they do and try to learn from their example. We are visual people; we learn by seeing as much as by hearing. Work hard to find good people to follow, because believe me, there is likely someone who is following you.

Third, expand your spiritual ability. We mark growth in maturity by milestones that are reached and skills that are mastered. Let me illustrate.

- We celebrate the first steps of our babies as a step toward mobility (which we will often lament for the next several years!)
- We listen for a child's first words because it shows they have reached a new level of communication.
- We mark the first day of school because it is a step forward in education and socialization.
- We note a first boyfriend or girlfriend because it indicates a new level of maturity.
- We celebrate (cautiously) the day our child gets their driver's license because they are taking a step toward independence.

These are all markers that signal a person is maturing. There are several milestones in Christian maturity:

- The development of a daily time with God.
- An honest and transparent awareness of sin and the desire to repent.
- Feeling comfortable sharing your faith with others.
- Beginning to give to the Lord cheerfully rather than out of duty.

- Trying to reach out to those who are hurting. It may be a mission trip. It may be taking in an abandoned or abused child. It may be a visit to someone at home or the hospital, it may be taking time to pray with someone facing a crisis, or it may be as simple as putting on your work clothes to pitch in to address a need. When compassion becomes practical rather than theoretical, maturity is beginning to show.
- Using our gifts in the building of God's Kingdom. This is when we stop asking what the church can do for me and begin looking for what we can contribute to the church.
- When we are willing to forgive the hurts in our past. In other words, when we choose to leave the hurt, bitterness, and resentment with the Lord and move beyond the pain.

These are like road signs that indicate we are headed in the right direction. Look for progress in your life. Pursue maturity diligently.

God doesn't expect a new believer to act like a mature believer. But He also doesn't expect someone who has followed Christ for awhile to continue to act like an infant. God wants us to grow, mature, contribute, and be an example of what Christ can and will do in the human heart.

Take a good look at your life. Evaluate your spiritual maturity and then instead of making excuses, start moving forward.

Dig Deeper

1. Would you classify most Christians you know as mature or immature? What makes you think this?
2. If you had a friend who recently declared faith in Christ and they asked you what to do so they would grow in faith and maturity, what would you tell him?
3. What milestones of maturity do you see in your own life? Which milestones seem a long way off?

Bruce and Rick Goettsche

4
The Best Way to Show Gratitude
Ephesians 4:17-24

Each year we designate one day as Thanksgiving. There are family dinners, parades, and football games. Hopefully, there will be a moment or two when we stop and express our thanks to the Lord.

The best way to show gratitude is not by declaring a holiday, it is by living a LIFE of gratitude.

We live in an age of "entitlement." We believe the government owes us, the school system owes us, the police owe us, and our employers owe us. We even think the church owes us a good time, a great music program and a powerful youth program in which we don't have to be involved. Sadly, we often also feel that God owes us a trouble free life, material abundance, and the fulfillment of all our dreams. We are better at demanding than we are at appreciating gifts of grace and blessing we have received.

In Ephesians 4:17-23 Paul tells us that there is a right way and a wrong way to show our gratitude to the Lord.

What Not to Do: Live Like Everyone Else

Just because we say we are thankful doesn't mean we are living as grateful people. Paul admonishes the Ephesians:

> *So I tell you this, and insist on it in the Lord, that you must no longer live as the Gentiles do, in the futility of their thinking. They are darkened in their understanding and separated from the life of God because of the ignorance that is in them due to the hardening of their hearts. Having lost all sensitivity, they have given themselves over to sensuality so as to*

indulge in every kind of impurity, with a continual lust for more. (Ephesians 4:17-19)

Paul says our previous way of life was futile. Listen to the way the New Living Translation states this,

Their minds are full of darkness; they wander far from the life God gives because they have closed their minds and hardened their hearts against him. They have no sense of shame. They live for lustful pleasure and eagerly practice every kind of impurity. (Ephesians 4:18-19, NLT)

The unbeliever has "closed their mind and hardened their hearts." Basically, they have ignored God so much that they no longer even hear His voice. They have concluded that their only truly reliable guide for life is their desires. They may be religious, but they are not interested in following the Lord; they are interested in getting the Lord to help them reach *their* goals and *their* agenda. Such people are not interested in truth...they are interested in vindication, validation, and victory! They don't feel grateful. More often than not, they feel cheated!

The book *The Marriage Miracle* suggests that the cause of most marriage breakups is actually this same kind of hardening of heart. One or both of the people become self-absorbed. They stop trying to understand and care for the other person. In other words, they stop working and simply give up. You might hear them say they have "fallen out of love," but the truth is, they have decided to stop working at love! This happens when all the focus is on needs the other person has failed to meet for me!

No one develops a hardened heart overnight in marriage or in any other area. The process begins when we ignore God's clear commands and begin to justify our sin. We convince ourselves that our behavior is not wrong, in spite of what the Bible says. This eventually numbs our spirit. As we continue to make excuses, we bury the truth deeper and become increasingly deaf to the whispers of God's Spirit. Eventually, our hearts become unresponsive to the ways of God.

John Stott, in his commentary on Ephesians noted the downward slide that happens when we start to harden our heart,

1) hardness of heart
2) darkness of heart
3) deadness
4) recklessness—unrestrained abandonment to sin.

The best example of this in the Bible is David with Bathsheba. He knew it was improper to lustfully watch a woman bathe, but he ignored the warning of the Spirit in his heart and mind. He ignored his conscience. He had to continue to "run through stop signs" for him to get the name of Bathsheba, and then send for her. This did not "just happen," it was a series of choices! His private sin became public and active and he didn't care! When Bathsheba was found to be pregnant, David was then able to justify the murder of Uriah, her husband, to himself. By marrying Bathsheba, David convinced himself that somehow he was "doing the right thing."

This is what Paul describes when he says, "Having lost all sensitivity, they have given themselves over to sensuality so as to indulge in every kind of impurity, with a continual lust for more." (v. 19)

The word for "sensuality" is the word *aselgeia* in the Greek. This is when a person no longer tries to hide their sin. They no longer care at all what others say. They are solely absorbed in their pleasure. Decency and shame disappear.

Look critically at what you see in movies, television and even some of the popular literature of today. It is obvious that people are not bothered by what God calls sin; they even want to celebrate and encourage what God calls sin in others!

All of these people may sit down and talk about their "blessings" at a Thanksgiving dinner, yet they are unwilling to submit or truly honor the One who does the blessing! Many people are only thankful that they are such fine people; and are so "open-minded" and progressive.

What TO Do

You, however, did not come to know Christ that way. Surely you heard of him and were taught in him in accordance with the truth that is in Jesus. You were taught, with regard to your former way of life, to put off your old self, which is being corrupted by its deceitful desires; to be made new in the attitude of your minds; and to put on the new self, created to be like God in true righteousness and holiness. (Ephesians 4:20-24)

Make Sure of Your Faith

Before we look at the specifics, notice something important: Paul is talking to those who have "come to know Christ." He is talking to believers; those who have turned to Christ for salvation and new life. These are people who have been made new by God's Spirit.

We will never truly honor God, we will never truly live a different life, until we are first *redeemed* people. As long as we refuse to bow before the Lord of life and accept the salvation and the new life that He offers, EVERYTHING we do is really an attempt to exclude Him from our lives; to make Him irrelevant. These are not words telling people to work harder, they are words to redeemed people telling them to live as those who have been redeemed!

Paul tells us to *put off the old self.* This is like the old joke where the patient says "Doctor, my arm hurts every time I lift it over my head." The Doctor responds, "Then stop lifting it over your head!" There are times when the first step toward godly living requires that we stop doing what is destroying us! We must put away the old life.

The notion that we can live comfortably in both worlds is wrong. Jesus said you can't serve two masters. We can't serve the world and the Kingdom of God at the same time because they are going in opposite directions! We must make a choice as to which direction we are going to go.

Paul says the first step to grateful living is to leave behind that which was destroying your life and your relationship with God. We all know that this is much easier said than done. There are some preliminary steps to leaving the past behind,

Acknowledge There is a Problem

Denial makes healing impossible. We must recognize that something is going wrong in our hearts and our lives. There are several steps we must take:

Face the reality of your sin. Don't blame it on others or on your circumstances. Don't blame your personality or even your "needs" (these seem to imply that God "made you this way"). Face the reality: you are rebelling against the clear instruction of our Holy God. You are refusing to submit to His rule in your life

Ask God (and those you have hurt) to forgive you. (Proverbs 15:9) True forgiveness and restoration requires we confess the specific sin and hurt of which we are guilty both to the Lord and to the one offended. We have a tendency to say, "Sorry!" and conclude that this "fixes" everything! Implying that a deep hurt can be fixed with a simple "sorry" is absurd and hurtful to the one offended. We must show that we understand what we have done and how it has affected the other person.

Rest in God's transformational mercy. Once we have squarely faced the wrong in our lives and confessed our sin, we must rest in the incredible and undeserved forgiveness of the Lord. Other people may or may not accept your apology, but if you have been sincere and specific, you have done what God requires and He will extend forgiveness. Embrace that forgiveness. Take Him at His Word.

Head in the new direction God has provided for you. In order to truly break with the past we may have to change some relationships, develop new interests, check into a treatment program, get counseling, or even get a different job. It all starts by facing the truth.

Change the Channel

The second step is to change the channel of your mind. When you are watching television, if you don't like what is on TV you simply "change the channel." This is what we need to do in our thinking. We are to be "made new" in the attitude of our minds. Here's what I mean,

- Rather than focusing on pleasing the crowd, focus on pleasing the Lord.
- Rather than dwelling on your hardship, choose to be thankful for blessings.
- Rather than complain about life, choose to sing.
- Rather than spotlight the faults of family members, enumerate and celebrate their strengths.
- Rather than list why you *can't* do something, choose to focus on ways you *can* do something.
- Rather than defending your self-image, choose to admit your weakness and failures in humility.
- Rather than choose to respond in anger, choose to respond with grace and mercy.
- Rather than choose to participate in the gossip, choose to defend the person or simply walk away.

Do you get the idea? You must change the channel of your mind! In the process, we must change what we feed our minds. One of the keys (I'm told) to weight loss and healthy living is eating differently. We must eat better and eat smarter. We can't keep feeding our body garbage and think that it will work at its optimum level. It's like putting sugar in a gas tank...eventually the engine will be destroyed.

If we feed on God's Word rather than on the schemes, propaganda, and whispers of the world, we will naturally begin to think differently. Imagine how your thinking would change if you turned off the TV for an hour and read from your Bible instead. What if you kept the radio tuned to Christian teaching and music rather than to talk radio or secular music? What if you made spending time with other believers a much higher priority in your life? What if you watched one or two less games and used that time to read a book that would enrich your walk with Christ? What would happen if you began to think and act differently?

Put on the New Self

The last step has to be the last step in the process: Put on the new self. You can't put on the new self until you have dealt with the old you.

As the old saying goes, "only a fool thinks they can keep doing the same thing and get a different result."

Charles Sheldon's classic "In His Steps," which was updated by his family and re-titled, "What Would Jesus Do" is about "putting on of the new self." Sheldon suggested in his novel that people approach every situation and choice by asking, "What would Jesus do in this situation?"…and then doing it.

There are some who respond to this notion of asking, "What does God want me to do?" by saying, "I don't know what God wants me to do." Let me be direct. I don't think that is true! I believe we do know what God wants us to do...you just don't want to do it! It is easier to say you "didn't know" than admit we refuse to obey.

It's God's voice that is calling you to
- Forgive an offense
- Stand up for the Truth of God's Word
- Let go of a hurt
- Give more than what is "comfortable"
- Help someone in need
- Love someone who is hard to love
- Talk to a friend who does not know Christ
- Move in a different direction

Instead of ignoring God's way (and developing a hardness in our heart) Paul calls us to listen and to follow.

What Does this Have to Do with Gratitude?

Suppose you knew that someone needed transportation to work. They needed to be able to take their kids to school and run the errands that come with life. So, as an act of Christian generosity and compassion you gave that person a car. The family cried when you gave them the keys. They sent you a very nice thank you note. Every week on Sunday they went out to the garage and looked at and admired the car. Sometimes they even sat in it. Once a year they invited their friends over to have a party in honor of the car in the garage. They talk about how the car has changed their life...but they never take it out of the garage! They still need transportation!

Here's the question: Would you feel good about the gift? You would not. You gave the car so it would be driven.

There is a parallel. God saw our great need and sent Christ to die so that we might be delivered from the darkness and be able to walk in the light. Jesus came so we could be delivered from the bondage of the past and set free to walk in a new direction. He gave us new life so we could actually live a new way!

If you really want to show gratitude for what God has given to you, then use His gift! Don't simply talk about how great the gift is; use it! Allow God's grace to change the way you live. If you want to show real gratitude, embrace the life Christ offers and let Him lead you in a new direction. Let God soften your heart and change your life.

Jesus has opened the door to us for new life. The people who truly appreciate His gift don't simply admire the door or even what appears to be beyond the door. They walk through the door into the life He died to make possible.

Thanksgiving Day is a holiday. But true gratitude is something that is reflected every day in the way we live our lives. May God help us to hear His voice, follow His way, and demonstrate just how grateful we really are.

Dig Deeper

1. How would you define gratitude?
2. Why do you think it is so difficult to live differently than the rest of the world?
3. Of the three steps (Acknowledge there is a problem; Change the channel; and Put on the new self) which do you find the hardest to do consistently?
   a. Why do you think this is so?
   b. What practical steps can you take to develop greater consistency?
4. Did you find the car illustration helpful? Why are we reluctant to "drive the car"?

5
Telling the Truth in A World of Deception
Ephesians 4:25

Sometimes you hear the statement that Christians are so "heavenly minded they are no earthly good." It is a devastating criticism charging believers with always talking about faith but never applying their faith in a way which makes any kind of difference in their day to day living.

The criticism sadly, is not without merit. We have all met people who go to church, can tell you all the signs of the Second coming of Jesus, can argue points of theology, and are always telling others about their strong faith. However, they also can't be trusted in business, are among the biggest gossips, are mean to the members of their family, and always seem to be in a grumpy mood. These people do more harm than good for the Kingdom of God.

The thing I appreciate about the book of Ephesians is that it strikes a balance between knowledge and practice. Paul tells us that we must "walk in a manner worthy of the gospel" (4:1). He reminds us God has not called us to serve Him in isolation but to serve Him in community. We all have a part to play in the family of Christ. Because of this, he tells us we must live differently than unbelievers. Instead of being led by urges, we should be led by truth. Instead of being hard, we should be soft.

Paul is now going to become more specific. Since I like to make lists to help me apply general principles to real situations, I like to think that this is what Paul is doing in the verses ahead. He warns us of what not to do (the behavior of the sinful world), and then tells us what we should do (the behavior of a true follower), and why we should do these things.

Some Things to Remember

Before we get into the first item on Paul's list it is important we understand some things about this list. First, keep in mind that Paul never says it will be easy to do these things. We must *grow* in Godliness. To some degree, we will always be working on the things Paul lists here. However, even though we may never do these things perfectly, we should be able to see progress over the course of time.

Second, we must not mistake what Paul is telling us. He is not merely saying we need to be "better people." This is what we hear from everyone: "Work harder!" "Get your act together!" "Take charge of your life!" Theologically this is called "moralism," the belief that we can "save ourselves." Paul tells us to live the life that is possible through a surrender of our lives to the way of the Spirit.

D. Martyn Lloyd-Jones does a good job of showing the difference between moralism and living the life of the Spirit. He says,

> *Moralism is more about cultural norms rather than divine truth. Being a "good person" is about appearing good in the eyes of others. God's truth calls us to some behaviors that are counter-cultural. God is concerned about character not just behavior.*

> *Moralism assumes that we can be good. That is a very hard message to those who struggle. Lloyd-Jones says, "this kind of faith has nothing to offer failures." The world seems to say: you must fix yourself. The gospel however says we are all sinful people in need of the undeserved grace of God. Every one of us needs a new beginning. This is why sometimes the people most enthusiastic to embrace the gospel are those who have failed greatly. Christ is the only One who offers them any real hope.*

> *The notion of "being a good person" promotes self-satisfaction and pride. If we achieve a reputation as a "good person" we can feel pleased with ourselves and our achievements and even our religious*

superiority while still missing the internal transformation God desires.

Simply trying to "Be Good" tends to leave the sinful heart untouched; we simply whitewash the person. It regulates outbreaks but doesn't do anything about the vice itself.

Being good is more about repressing our old self than it is about living in a new self.⁵

What Paul talks about here is not reformation, it is transformation! He is not calling us to be better...but to be a new person.

Now, let's get on to the specifics. The first specific characteristic Paul addresses is in verse 25

Therefore each of you must put off falsehood and speak truthfully to his neighbor, for we are all members of one body.

What to Stop Doing – Lying

We lie any time we twist, pervert, or bury what is true. We can lie by speaking, by not speaking up, and even by a look or a tone of voice.

There are different kinds of lying...

Exaggeration. We make things bigger or worse than they really are. We lie when we paint ourselves as being more significant than we actually are. An example is when we make ourselves the insightful one in the story. We present ourselves as the one with the pivotal insight, the perfect action, the hero. Most of the time, this is exaggeration.

Flattery (manipulating truth to get something). We say nice things to others not because they are true but because we hope that "buttering someone up" will make them more open to what we want them to do.

Misleading statements and Innuendo (implying something that may not be true) or other distortions of the truth. Just because we didn't overtly lie does not mean we have not implied a falsehood. Think about political ads. They find something a person said, take it out of context, and play it over and over to make the person sound like a buffoon. The response is: "you heard it in their own words...it is what they said!" It was what they said, but they have changed the meaning of what they were saying through distortion!

Gossip (passing on the half-truths or inappropriate truth others have shared with you). Gossip is one of the most devastating vices there is. It ruins reputations, separates friends, violates confidences, and can destroy families. It is a sharpened tool of the Devil. Christians are known to justify gossip by saying they are "sharing a prayer concern."

Drawing conclusions from "facts not in evidence." We do this all the time. Someone does something and we draw (and share) conclusions we have drawn from the actions. For example, we say "they said (or did) this and they meant it in a particular way." We know what they did, but we do not know their intention.

We have been gossiped about. Sometimes what was said was factual but out of context. It is easy to brand, demonize, and vilify someone if all you have is one side of the story.

Keeping silent about what you know is false. If a falsehood is being promoted and we say nothing, we are an accessory to a lie. We may be guilty of a lesser lie, but it is a lie nonetheless.

Claiming things are ours that actually belong to another. We see this in people who write papers they got from someone else and pass them off as their own. We see it when you take credit at work for something someone else did or an idea that someone else had. You can see it even in people who share stories that happened to another as if it happened to them!

Let's not kid ourselves; many of these things are acceptable practice in our world. For most of us, lying is an "unconscious survival technique." We lie to escape consequences or to make ourselves look better than we actually are.

How many times have you been in a situation where you did something and a person asks, "Did you do (or say) this?" And we respond, "No!" It is instinct. We want to avoid conflict or trouble. Kids do it all the time. You may actually observe them coloring on the walls of your house and ask, "Did you get this crayon all over the wall?" The child will look at you and say, "No, I didn't do that." Why? Because we are sinful people who want to protect ourselves.

We see this as far back as the Garden of Eden! Adam and Eve sidestepped the truth when talking with the Lord in an effort to avoid the consequences of their actions. Lying (of any kind) is an expression of the sinful nature that infects us all.

Sometimes lying will help us get ahead. If we inflate our importance, divert blame, or implicate others we can often get promoted. If we lie about our record or our finances we may be able to get a job, a loan, or even get hand-outs from the government. Paul tells us that this is not God's way—even though it seems to be the way of everyone around us. Lying only benefits us in the short-term, and it runs contrary to God's instructions for our lives.

What to Begin Doing – The Alternative

The believer is to be characterized by truth. This is more than simply "not telling a lie." To be a truth-teller means to maintain "fidelity to an original or standard." In other words, being a person of truth means telling the truth by our words *and* by our lives. It is to live by the standard of truthfulness.

Practically, telling the truth involves,

- Fulfilling our promises.
- Being careful about what we say.
- Speaking truthfully about others…sticking to facts without interpretation or exaggeration. Leaving room for the benefit of the doubt.
- Being honest about your failures and struggles rather than exaggerating your good traits.
- Being truthful in business dealings.
- Trying to understand both (or all) sides of an issue.
- Being honest with others about the need for a saving relationship with Jesus.

Paul said earlier that telling the truth is not simply blasting away at others. We are to "speak the truth in love." This is an important balance to maintain. Our job is to communicate the truth not simply blast away with it.

William Barclay says,

> *It is more from carelessness about truth than from intentional lying, that there is so much falsehood in the world.*"[6]

If we are going to be truth-tellers we must be careful with the truth. We should speak accurately and honestly. And we must be especially careful with the truth of Scripture. We should quote verses correctly and proclaim God's truth as accurately as possible. We do this because truth matters.

Why?

Paul is not content to give us mere directives. He wants us to understand why it is important to be a truth teller. He says we should tell the truth because "we are all members of one body."

Since we are members of the body of Christ we should reflect the character of our Savior and our God. In the beginning of the book of Titus (1:2) we are told that God does not lie. The implication is since God does not lie, we shouldn't either.

The first sin in the Garden of Eden (after eating from the tree) was a lie. Adam and Eve lied to God, and blamed others rather than accepting responsibility for what they'd done. Jesus said Satan was the "Father of Lies." In other words, when we tell the truth we are following the way of Christ; when we lie, we are following the path of the Devil.

Even in those times where we may "get away" with lying to others, God still sees the truth. **Once we start down the path of lying, one lie leads to another until you are so wrapped in lies that you don't know how to extricate yourself.** Lies complicate life and rob us of joy. We will always fret that we will be "found out." Jesus is giving us good counsel when He says the "truth will set us free."

Lying undermines your relationships. Lying undermines every relationship but Paul is concerned especially for our relationship with each other in the church. Once people conclude that you are not a truth-teller it is going to be hard to get anyone to consider anything you say as credible.

In order to grow in grace and truth we need to be honest with each other. As a Christian community we are to be anchored in the truth. The only way we can flourish and grow is if we are honest about our needs, our struggles, and our conflict with each other. Instead of talking about each other, we need to talk TO each other. Sure it is hard! It is always easier to talk *about* people. However, love starts with honesty.

Conclusion

Truthfulness is not valued like it once was. We seem to view lies as necessary to keeping peace, getting ahead, and keeping customers happy. You may even hear some say, "The truth is whatever you want it to be." As a result, our society is adrift. We have become more cynical, suspicious and antagonistic because by default we seem to believe that people are lying to us. We believe everyone is working some kind of a scam. Many of the lawsuits we see today are because people instinctively believe there is a cover-up of some sort going on.

We can wring our hands about the state of our society, or we can see an opportunity. We have an opportunity to show by contrast what it means to be a Christ-follower. We have the opportunity to point people to the One who is True. The only way to do this is to anchor our own lives to truth. We must show people a better way.

How do we start? Here are some simple suggestions. **Examine your words.** Pursue truthfulness in all that you say. Be truthful and accurate about facts. If you lost 6 pounds don't say you've lost 10, if you ran 1 ½ miles, don't say that you ran 2 miles. If you only skimmed a book, don't say you read it. If you made extra money on the side, be honest and report it. If you are struggling in your spiritual life, be honest rather than pretending. Determine to be truthful in everything you say. If we will pursue honesty in the little things we will find it much easier to be honest in the bigger things.

Search for Truth in what you hear. In the book of Acts we read about the Bereans who heard the words of Paul and then checked them out. They wanted to know the truth not merely a person's opinion.

We need to be people who are always looking for the "rest of the story." Check facts. Look at the counter argument (you haven't really checked facts until you understand both sides of the argument). Let me give you an example. Rather than assuming the worst about someone; concluding the gossip or innuendo is true; check it out. I have had really good success saying to people, "I don't know if you know this or not but this is what is being said about you...what is going on?" There is *always* another side of the story and people appreciate the fact that you want to hear it.

This is actually a good discipline for us personally. As we learn to examine the facts about others thoroughly, we will start to examine the facts we tell ourselves more fully as well. Frankly, we often lie to ourselves. We need to monitor and evaluate our "self-talk."

Be honest (but gentle) about hard things. When you see someone heading in a bad direction, honestly tell them that you are concerned. When you believe someone is wrong in their thinking it is a good idea to say, "I guess I see that issue from a different perspective. Would you like to hear how I understand things?" If we are gentle, we can be truthful (and remain friends), even in awkward situations.

Relay the message of the Gospel truthfully. We don't have to be mean or abusive. We should not come off sounding arrogant. We should not seem like we are happy that someone might be heading to Hell and Judgment. At the same time, we dare not water down the truth of the gospel. There is only ONE way of salvation and that is through trusting and surrendering to the person and work of Jesus Christ. We must not veer from the true message of the gospel. A changed gospel message is a false gospel message!

There is nothing kind or loving about withholding the truth of the gospel from others. We say we are silent because we don't want to offend others. Here's the question: Which is ultimately more offensive: telling someone the truth so they might repent and find new life in Christ; or compromising the truth so someone feels good about their situation with God while they head to eternal destruction?

The truth has eternal consequences. The Lord of truth reminds us that we will give account for every idle word. The next time you are tempted to lie to escape the awkwardness of the moment, remember the Lord is watching and taking note.

Dig Deeper

1. What kinds of lies mentioned in this chapter surprised you?
2. Explain a time you were hurt by a lie.
3. What Biblical examples of lying can you think of?
4. Why do you think we lie so easily?
5. Which kind of lying is the biggest struggle for you?
6. Why is lying incompatible with living as a child of God?
7. Which of the practical suggestions do you think will be most helpful? Why?

Bruce and Rick Goettsche

6
Controlling Anger
Ephesians 4:26-27

Paul takes us next to a subject that has touched most every life in one way or another. We have all been bruised by the angry words of others and we likely have bruised a few people along the way by our own angry words. Anger is a powerful emotion and how we deal with this emotion will impact our relationships, our attitude toward life, and even our witness before a watching world.

The Book of Proverbs has much to say about anger.

- Psalm 37:8 Refrain from anger and turn from wrath; do not fret—it leads only to evil.
- Proverbs 12:16 A fool shows his annoyance at once, but a prudent man overlooks an insult.
- Proverbs 12:18 Reckless words pierce like a sword, but the tongue of the wise brings healing.
- Proverbs 16:32 Better a patient man than a warrior, a man who controls his temper than one who takes a city.
- Proverbs 19:19 A hot-tempered man must pay the penalty; if you rescue him, you will have to do it again.

The New Testament tells us to get rid of anger. It says true love is not "easily angered." James tells us to be slow to anger. With all these commands in mind we may be surprised at this command from the Apostle Paul,

> *"In your anger do not sin": Do not let the sun go down while you are still angry, and do not give the devil a foothold. (Ephesians 4:26-27)*

Good Anger

What makes this passage especially interesting is the fact that it begins with this quote from Psalm 4:4 "In your anger, do not sin." Paul does not say we should never get angry. Anger is an emotion that has its proper place (like all emotions). Anger in and of itself is not bad. Anger is like a river that is only bad when it escapes its banks or becomes contaminated by poison.

There are times we should be angry. Moses was angry at the sin of the people; the prophets were angry at the obstinacy of the people; Jesus became angry at those who victimized or misled others; and we are told that God will reveal His just wrath (which is a type of anger). Proper anger is directed at wrong behavior and those who facilitate or encourage wrong behavior. We should be angry at that which destroys others or offends the character or Kingdom of God.

Martyn Lloyd-Jones now sounds prophetic when he wrote,

> It is a sad reality that we have chosen to simply ignore wrong and sin. In fact, the whole category of "sinful behavior" is being attacked. The only "evil" is that which stands in the way of what I want in my life! This should anger us because it is an offense to God and it is destroying us and those around us! A failure to feel angry at such things is a sign of a pagan society.

Even the former chairman of the Chrysler Corporation, Lee Iacocca, understood this fact. When addressing the graduating class at the University of Michigan, in 1983 he said:

> I want you to get mad about the current state of affairs. I want you to get so mad that you kick your elders in their figurative posteriors and move America off dead center. Our nation was born when 56 patriots got mad enough to sign the Declaration of Independence. We put a man on the moon because Sputnik made us mad at being No. 2 in space. Getting

> *mad in a constructive way is good for the soul—and*
> *the country.*[7]

I can hear Paul saying similar words to the church: It is time to get mad enough at the current state of affairs that we actually begin to DO something

Anger is a valuable emotion because it alerts us to a problem that needs to be addressed. We become angry when we feel pushed aside, taken advantage of, or when we see that someone is being inconsiderate or self-absorbed. We get angry when we see destructive things happening in the life of another. We get angry when others are being treated unfairly.

But it is important to note something. Jesus got angry when others were victimized or pushed aside. He was angry when people trampled on the law of God. He was angry when truth was distorted. Jesus did not get angry when someone insulted Him or called Him names. He *discussed and debated* these actions but He did not get angry. We are told Jesus was angry two times,

- Jesus was angry that the disciples were keeping the children from Him (Mark 10:14).
- Jesus was angry when he went to visit Mary and Martha after the death of Lazarus (John 11:33, 38). Many believe Jesus was angry because of the unbelief in the people even as they "comforted" Mary and Martha.

We usually conclude Jesus was angry when he drove the people out of the temple courts. However, the Bible does not say he was angry. We assume he was because he made a whip and drove them out.

Perhaps you could say his anger was directed at righting wrongs rather than defending Himself.

We have turned that around. We quickly become offended when we believe we have not been treated fairly but have little response when we see evil toward others or disrespect toward God.

Brant Hansen, in his wonderful and eye-opening book, *Unoffendable*, cautions us about concluding our anger is righteous.

In the moment, everyone's anger always seems righteous. Anger is a feeling, after all, and it sweeps over us and tells us we're being denied something we should have. It provides its own justification. But an emotion is just an emotion. It's not critical thinking. Anger doesn't pause. We have to stop, and we have to question it. We humans are experts at casting ourselves as victims and rewriting narratives that put us in the center of injustices. And we can repaint our anger or hatred of someone—say, anyone who threatens us—into a righteous-looking work of art.[8]

Hansen continues,

In the Bible's "wisdom literature," anger is always—not sometimes, always—associated with foolishness, not wisdom. The writer recognized that, yes, anger may visit us, but when it finds a residence, it's "in the lap of fools" (Eccl. 7: 9). Let that sink in. When anger lives, that's where it lives: in the lap of a fool. Thinking we're entitled to keep anger in our laps—whether toward the sin of a political figure, a news network, your dumb neighbor, your lying spouse, your deceased father, whomever—is perfectly natural, and perfectly foolish. Make no mistake. Foolishness destroys. Being offended is a tiring business. Letting things go gives you energy.[9]

The Destructive Effects of Anger

Anger is a powerful emotion. It is easy for anger to turn sinful. Sinful anger is mean, personally hurtful, or abusive. Sinful anger often results in rage or a loss of control. When anger (or any emotion) controls our life, we are in trouble. Godly anger is always a controlled anger.

People handle anger in several inappropriate ways. First, **we suppress anger.** We conclude all anger is wrong so we stuff our angry feelings. Unfortunately, the problem not only does not get resolved (so it continues to grind and wear on us), but anger can only be stuffed for so long before it either explodes (often over something minor), eats us up and destroys us physically or emotionally, or expresses itself in bitterness, a contentious spirit, or a negative attitude.

We spew. These people are always "getting things off their chest." They express their anger and feel better but give little thought to the collateral damage they do. They assault others with their words and actions and excuse themselves by saying, "this is just the way I am." They tend to rely on intimidation to get their way. They seem to know their anger keeps others off balance and like that sense of control. They may do great harm to others and excuse it by saying that they are only being honest.

> *Alexander the Great was one of the few men in*
> *history who seemed to deserve his descriptive title.*
> *He was energetic, versatile, and intelligent. Although*
> *hatred was not generally part of his nature, several*
> *times in his life he was tragically defeated by anger.*
> *The story is told of one of these occasions, when a*
> *dear friend of Alexander, a general in his army,*
> *became intoxicated and began to ridicule the*
> *emperor in front of his men. Blinded by anger and*
> *quick as lightning, Alexander snatched a spear from*
> *the hand of a soldier and hurled it at his friend.*
> *Although he had only intended to scare the drunken*
> *general, his aim was true and the spear took the life*
> *of his childhood friend.*
>
> *Deep remorse followed his anger. Overcome with*
> *guilt, Alexander attempted to take his own life with*
> *the same spear, but he was stopped by his men. For*
> *days he lay sick, calling for his friend and chiding*
> *himself as a murderer. He had conquered many*
> *cities and vanquished many countries, but he had*
> *failed miserably to control his own spirit.*[10]

Will Rogers said it well: "People who fly into a rage always make a bad landing."

The third inappropriate way of handling anger is by being **passive-aggressive.** In this case we find ways to express our anger in more subtle ways that make us feel we are "controlling our anger." This often comes out through gossip, manipulation, sarcasm, snide comments, a negative outlook or even silence. Passive Aggressive behavior leads us to "punish people" rather than pursue resolution to disagreements. We snip at each other rather than actually address the issue at hand. We believe we are under control but in reality our anger is poisoning almost everything we do.

The Reasons We Must Control Anger

Nothing good comes from unproductive anger. Frederick Buechner writes,

> *Of the seven deadly sins, anger is possibly the most fun. To lick your wounds, to smack your lips over grievances long past, to roll over your tongue the prospect of bitter confrontation still to come, to savor to the last toothsome morsel both the pain you are given and the pain you are giving back; in many ways it is a feast fit for a king. The chief drawback is that what you are wolfing down is yourself. The skeleton at the feast is you.[11]*

Paul says when we allow anger to control us we are actually inviting the Devil into our lives. Anger will give the Devil a foothold. The Devil will use anger to destroy relationships, families, and churches. Someone has said, holding on to anger and bitterness makes as much sense as drinking poison in the hope that it will kill your enemy! Even if you keep your anger hidden from others…it will still destroy you!

How We Control Anger

The question then is: How do we control our anger rather than let it control us? As a fellow traveler on this road let me make a few suggestions that I hope will help us get a handle on this deadly emotion.

Embrace Your Position in Christ. This may be the most helpful aspect of dealing with anger. Much of our anger comes from feeling that we have been treated as if we were insignificant (think about our annoyance at the waitress who doesn't seem to notice us). We are insecure and afraid of being rejected. In these times we need to remind ourselves of several things

1. No matter what the world says or does, God sees us, knows us, and loves us. We need to remember that we ARE significant in Christ whether or not the world around us recognizes it.
2. God calls us to be forgiving and loving. That does not mean we have to be a doormat, but it should mean we are always kind and gracious to others. God has told us to trust Him to vindicate us.
3. God calls us to a humility that recognizes we are sinners saved by grace. We too annoy others. We do things that are selfish and myopic. Just as we are people in need of growth and grace, so it is with those who frustrate us.

Be Aware of Anger Beginning to Rise. The first key to handling anger is to deal with it before it is out of control. Be aware of when your breathing starts getting faster or you start to feel the warmth of flush. Try to recognize your anger when it is at the stage of mild aggravation rather than full scale irritation. This is when we need to take action.

Stop and Consider the Story You Are Telling Yourself. Between a person's act and our response to that act, there is a story that we tell ourselves. It is so quickly told that we are usually unaware of it. We draw conclusions about

*   What the words of a person *really* mean
*   What their body language is saying
*   What their intentions and motives are
*   How that person feels about us

Let me give you a simple example. If someone says to you, "Wow, you look nice" you can interpret it as someone saying, "You look very nice I would like to get to know you better," or "You look nice…for a change," or "Wow, you actually look nice…who knew?" How you *interpret* those words has a big impact on how you respond to them.

We are always telling ourselves some story; most of the time it is unconscious. We need to understand the story we are telling ourselves. It is of course possible that all the person was doing was making a casual observation that had no overtones at all!

This is what happens when we react negatively to something someone said. When you sense anger beginning to rise, stop and ask what story you are telling yourself. What assumptions are you making? We should not trust our assumptions! Go back to what was actually said and calmly ask for clarification rather than prejudging the intentions and feelings of another.

Identify the Source of Your Response. It is helpful to ask, "Why am I angry?" The anger that gets us into trouble is always the result of some kind of pain. There are three common reasons for anger:

1. Hurt. Did something happen that makes you feel rejected, ignored, or pushed aside? Are you close to tears?
2. Fear. Do you feel threatened? Do you feel something is threatening your marriage, your well-being, or even your job? Do you feel your spouse is threatening you with divorce? Do you feel your fist clenching?
3. Frustration. Are things going differently than you had hoped, planned for, or expected? Is someone responding differently from what you hoped? Sometimes it is a delay, an illness, weather, car problems. These frustrations can lead to anger simply because our plans have been impacted. Sometimes (for me) the wrench that was your friend earlier is suddenly flying across the room.

It is much more productive to deal with the *cause* of our anger than trying to deal with the outburst itself. Once you understand *why* you are angry you can deal with the real issue behind the anger. Rather than saying you are angry (which puts us in combat mode) it is better to say, "I am hurt/afraid/frustrated." This will usually elicit the response, "Why?" which starts you on the process of understanding rather than war.

In the first case we would become defensive; ready for battle. In the second case we react with compassion. We want to help alleviate the pain. The goal is to focus on the pain not the response to it!

Deal with Anger Immediately. Paul tells us not to let the sun go down on our anger. The reason for this is that anger tends to burrow deep. The longer we wait the more bitter we become. The more bitter and resentful we are, the less rational we will be in dealing with the anger. The less rational we are the less chance of dealing with our anger effectively.

We must deal with things as quickly as possible. Bring it first to the Lord. Confess your angry, bitter, and revenge-filled feelings. Commit the "offender" to the Lord who died for him/her just as He did for you. With this new attitude we can then go to the person and try to work things out.

Take Responsibility for Your Anger and Choose to Release it. It is easy to blame others for our angry outbursts. However, other people do not *make* us angry. We choose (however unconsciously) to respond to another in anger. There are times when we have legitimately been wronged. We can choose to respond differently. We can ask ourselves: What kind of person do I want to be? Do I want to be one that quickly flies off the handle or one who listens, learns and tries to treat others with kindness and respect? We can ask: What response will leave me a healthy person?

Believe it or not we can choose to release our anger (though we will likely have to make that choice again and again). Dr. Les Carter lists signs that we have released anger.

- You show a genuine tolerance for others' flaws or weaknesses
- You choose to set aside a critical spirit, becoming fair-minded
- You give priority to forgiveness (rather than "victory")
- You choose kindness, even if others have not earned it
- You stay out of fruitless debate or discussion
- You accept the truth that you cannot expect life to give you everything you want
- You allow another to make a mistake
- You drop the requirement that others must do what you would like them to do.[12]

Finally, **Look for the Positive.** We have a choice: we can look for a fight or look for a blessing. We can focus on the faults or the gifts that reside in another. Choose to focus on positive things.

We live in an angry world. If we respond to angry people in kind, we will simply stoke the fires of hostility. That fire is already hot enough! Controlling anger will enrich our relationships, allow our families to grow in a healthy way, enhance our Christian witness, and help us to enjoy the journey of life. And who knows? Maybe we can help lead our society toward respect and kindness rather than hate and violence.

Dig Deeper

1. Think of examples of times when you became angry because of hurt, because of fear, or because of frustration. What were you hurt, afraid, or frustrated about?
2. Which of the three emotions that often lead to anger is the one that most often triggers anger in you?
3. What do you think is the difference between becoming angry at wrong or injustice (good anger), and sinful anger?
4. Which of the suggestions for controlling your anger do you find most helpful?

7
Doing Something Useful
Ephesians 4:28

Paul instructed the people in Ephesus (and by extension, all believers) that as followers of Christ, we should not live like everyone else. We are to "put off the old self" and live like people who have been given not only new life but also a new heart, outlook, and motivation.

Paul illustrated this new approach to life with a series of examples. He told us to put away lies and be people characterized by truthfulness. He said we should be angry but not sin. We are to be angry for the things which anger God and controlled and understanding at other times, because we realize how easy it is for Satan to use anger to lead us into sinful and hurtful practices.

Now Paul gives us another practical command:

> *He who has been stealing must steal no longer, but must work, doing something useful with his own hands, that he may have something to share with those in need. (Ephesians 4:28)*

Stop Stealing

The eighth commandment states it clearly: "Thou shalt not steal." Many of the people in the Ephesian Church came out of a very worldly background (much like us). They were used to "appropriating" things for themselves that belonged to another. Paul says such behavior must stop. The Greek word for "stealing" is klepto. This is where we get our word kleptomaniac—which is a person who steals small things incessantly.

> *Several years ago, A paper given at an American Psychological Association symposium on employee theft presented a breakdown on the 8 billion dollars that inventory shortages cost department and chain stores every year. Of these losses, 10 percent were due to clerical error, 30 percent to shoplifting, and a*

*shocking 60 percent (sixteen million dollars a day!)
to theft by employees.*[13]

I suspect that figure may be even higher now. Think about all the money that is now spent on security cameras, security personnel, and anti-theft devices! Even with all of this theft is on the rise.

Before you conclude this admonition doesn't apply to you, let's define stealing. There are different kinds of stealing.

Overt (Obvious) Theft

- Breaking into someone's home, garage, barn, car and taking something that belongs to another
- Writing bad checks
- Using stolen credit cards
- Shoplifting
- Not paying child support
- Taking items from a hotel or motel
- Plagiarizing someone's work or making a copy (or using bootlegged copies) of copyrighted software, music, or videos

Covert (Hidden) Theft

- Under-reporting your income
- Paying people in cash so neither of you has to report it to the government
- Making false (or inflated) insurance claims
- Taking money for a job you did not do
- Refusing to abide by the contract you agreed to
- Borrowing money you don't intend to (or can't) pay back
- Suing others over distorted or spurious losses

Business Theft

- Goofing off on the job
- Abusing an expense account
- Not paying your employees a fair wage
- Charging excessive interest

- Hiding money in dummy corporations
- Leaving work early
- Taking money from the company (embezzlement)
- Selling something and not recording the sale so you can pocket the cash
- Mismanagement of public funds
- Using work time to do personal (or even religious) things

Spiritual Theft

- Withholding our tithe. In the book of Malachi we are told that those who do not bring their tithe to the temple, are actually "Robbing God"
- Not using our spiritual gifts (this handicaps or steals from, the body of Christ)
- Not giving God glory or taking credit for God's work
- Absenting ourselves from worship which is stealing from others the benefit that your presence brings

Some argue that many kinds of theft are victimless crimes, but we all pay because of the theft of others. Those who don't report their income accurately necessitate more taxes. Spurious lawsuits lead to higher costs of insurance which also gets passed on to others. Stealing from God handicaps the work of God's people. Stealing is NOT a victimless crime.

Do Something Useful

Why is theft so prevalent? I can think of two reasons. The first is *our selfish nature.* Have you watched two little kids who are playing? How often do you see a child who is not interested in a particular toy until someone else picks it up to play with it? Immediately you hear those famous words: "Mine!" That attitude doesn't change over time (unless God does something in us). We are more subtle, but the attitude remains the same: we feel we should have what others have.

Not only do we feel we should have what others have, we feel we *deserve* what others have. As a result we feel *entitled* to what we have not earned. This is the problem we now face with what are called "entitlements." People view government aid as benefits to which they are entitled.

The Bible says, "The person who does not work should not eat" (2 Thessalonians 3:10). In other words, lazy people should not be rewarded. There are people who, due to no fault of their own, need extra help. There are those who are survivors of disaster, those who were suddenly laid off by places of business, those who cannot work because of physical or emotional problems, those who don't have enough to provide healthy things for their children, those who have overwhelming medical bills which they cannot pay; and who cannot work any longer but have no way of paying their own way. These people are the ones we should be trying to help.

There is a second problem: *We have failed to appreciate the value of hard work.* When Adam was placed in the Garden of Eden he was to "work and keep the garden." This was before sin ever entered the world. This is significant because it shows fruitful labor was part of God's perfect plan of creation. After the fall labor became more difficult and tedious, but labor itself is not bad, it is a good thing.

Paul exhorts us to "do something useful so you have something to share with others." Notice the purpose of work. It is not so we can feel good about ourselves or even so we can indulge ourselves (have more stuff). This tends to be the view that most people have. They want a good job so they can have more and do more. Paul urges us to work hard so that we are able to contribute to the world and help others.

To do this you don't need a high-salaried or glamorous job. The challenge is to do something "useful" that will contribute to the Kingdom of God in some way. The way we work and the reason we work is an offering to the Lord who made us.

If we understand the value of hard work several things happen.

- We will respect the property of others by not taking what doesn't belong to us and taking care of and returning things we borrow from another.
- Students, business people, and even Pastors will study, think, read, and write rather than merely pass on the work that someone else has done. We will spend more time on our knees in prayer seeking God's wisdom and less time running after the latest gimmick that guarantees success.

- We will define ourselves (and others) less by our job title and more by how well we serve the Lord IN our job. In other words we will draw our sense of significance not from what we do, but from the One we serve (the Lord).
- We will continue to work at relationships rather than toss them aside when they become difficult or tiresome. We will do this because we understand that some of the best things come from diligent labor.
- "Retirement" will be seen less as the end of our working life but rather as a time when we can serve the Lord in a different manner than we did before.
- We will see service to the Lord as more than simply dropping a check in the offering and more as a way of life.
- We will be less focused on material possessions and more on how we can use what we have to serve others.

One commentator writes,

> *What a challenging sign of newness of life. No more preoccupation with "building bigger barns," and accumulating huge estates to leave to our children when we die. No more frantic activity at the expense of what really counts—human tenderness, family love, and togetherness. No more compulsive earning and spending as victims of a consumer society.*[14]

The Biblical challenge is to be givers rather than takers.

Where Do We Start?

Paul encourages us to have a mindset that is quite different from the prevalent mindset in our society. How do we get there? Here are a few ideas.

Stop stealing. We need to examine our lives. Are we doing things that are actually stealing from others? Are we justifying the misuse of funds, misrepresenting income, cheating our employer? Are we robbing God? Are our priorities askew? Has our job become our life rather than a tool in life? Do we feel that we are entitled to handouts? We must ask these kinds of questions to identify any problem areas. We need to call these things what they are (rather than making excuses) and then take corrective action. You may need to right past wrongs or make some restitution. Do what you need to do to make things right.

Work Hard. Whatever you do, do it well. Serve the Lord whether it is doing dishes or running a corporation. Strive to be the best employee, the best boss, the best company there is. Don't do this out of a sense of competition...do it out of a desire to honor the One who has given you forgiveness and new life. In 1 Thessalonians 4 Paul writes, "You should mind your own business and work with your hands...so that your daily life may win the respect of outsiders and so that you will not be dependent on anybody."

However, let me caution you: doing many things is not the same as doing things well. Sometimes we can be so committed that we aren't doing anything well. The old saying is true: quality is more important than quantity. If you feel you can't do what is important because there are too many "urgent" things, you need to simplify your life! Rather than trying to do everything, we should be seeking to do the BEST things.

Beware of those who will resent your diligence. They may feel you are disrupting the status quo. At this point you need to ask whether you are serving the status quo or serving the Lord. Pursue excellence.

Change your attitude toward work. Instead of living for retirement, determine to work and serve the Lord for as long as you are able. Instead of hoarding for the future, use what you have to lead others to Christ. Look at your labor not as a necessary evil but as the area where you have been called to serve the Lord. There is truth to the adage that "idle hands are the Devil's workshop." Don't allow the Devil that opportunity!

Appreciate and give thanks for what you have. One of the ways to combat the attitude of entitlement is to cultivate an attitude of contentment. Contentment is learning to be grateful with what God has provided rather than feeling deprived.

Practically this means instead of wishing you had a different job, be grateful for the job you have. Instead of imagining a different family, celebrate the family you have. Instead of envying the home of another, cherish the character and memories that you have in your home. Instead of grumbling about the task at hand be grateful that you have a practical way in which you can show your love to God.

Look for practical ways to be of help to others. We can contribute in many ways without money. We can contribute to society even if we are not working for a paycheck. In fact, much of the help that is needed has little to do with money and more to do with time and a little creativity.

For example, you could

- Help someone learn a new trade so they can get a job.
- Offer to babysit while someone gets a needed education.
- Read to someone who can no longer read for themselves.
- Help someone with needed repairs.
- Volunteer as a listener in an Awana program.
- Serve in the Nursery at your church so parents can better concentrate in worship.
- Stop in to visit with someone who is alone.
- Drive someone to an appointment or take them shopping.

My mom didn't drive. Consequently, getting to appointments, the grocery store, and other places was a real problem for her. My Mom was blessed by a man named Phil. Phil is a Christian who has made it his "job" to offer a service to people like my mom. For a modest fee he came to get her every Monday and he took her shopping and then ran errands with her. He sometimes even took her to Doctors' appointments. To Phil this was not just a job, it was his ministry. When Phil tells others what he does, I'm sure it doesn't sound very glamorous. However, he is making a big difference. He is using what he has to serve others. He was a godsend to our family.

Here's the point: God has designed us to be productive members of His creation. In a sense, He calls us to be His hands, His feet, and His mouth in the world. He didn't send us to merely sit in churches and have endless meetings. He wants us to be willing vessels He works through to change the world.

The world places an emphasis on getting all we can for ourselves. Paul challenges us to focus on contributing to society and to others. We do this by engaging in fruitful labor and by working in a way that honors the Lord rather than simply growing our bank account. This work we are given to do is not a burden! It is actually something that will give us a true sense of significance and tremendous satisfaction. It is to be a joyful labor. Let us serve the Lord with gladness.

Dig Deeper

1. Why are we told not to steal?
2. Can you add any examples of stealing in today's world? Which of the examples listed surprised you?
3. How do you tell the difference between someone in need and someone who is "working the system?"
4. What are some additional areas where we can "be useful" serving the Lord? (Make a list of these ideas and share them with your church).

8
Rotten Talk
Ephesians 4:29

Once I went to eat at someone's house, and they had prepared a beautiful (and delicious) meal. Part of that meal was a bowl of fresh berries. They were absolutely beautiful and looked delicious. There is something attractive about fruit that is perfectly ripe. It has a beautiful color and looks enticing, whether you like that particular kind of fruit or not. Contrast that with fruit that has begun to rot. Fruit that shows signs of rot is anything but appetizing—rotten fruit is discarded because it actually does more harm than good.

What is interesting about rotting fruit is it has the ability to affect good fruit. Fruit that is in the process of going bad gives off ethylene gas, which speeds the process of ripening in other fruit that may be nearby. It will not just cause fruit to ripen; once it's ripened it will move quickly toward rotting. Rotten fruit brings about more rotten fruit.

In this one verse the apostle Paul uses the analogy of rotting fruit to instruct us about our conversation. Paul emphasized that our speech does not only impact us, it also impacts those around us. When we engage in talk that is rotten, it has a negative impact on others. When we engage in talk that builds up others, it has a positive impact.

What Not to Do

We turn to Ephesians 4:29,

> *Do not let any unwholesome talk come out of your mouths, but only what is helpful for building others up according to their needs, that it may benefit those who listen. (Ephesians 4:29)*

The Greek word that is translated "unwholesome" here has to do with rotting fruit. In essence, Paul is saying, "Don't let anything that causes rot and decay come out of your mouths."

We understand how words can have this effect, don't we? All of us have had the experience of being wounded by the words of others. You can probably recall some specific instances in your life when someone said something that hurt you deeply. Sometimes people say things that intentionally wound:

- You'll never amount to anything
- You're stupid
- You're ugly
- You are worthless
- You are a disappointment
- I have never loved you

These verbal darts can pierce our hearts and can leave us with deep wounds and scars that we carry around for years. People can wound us with their words on purpose, and sometimes words hurt us even when people aren't trying to do so. Here are a couple examples of ways in which people can unintentionally wound with their words.

- Why haven't you gotten married yet? (implying there must be something wrong with you if you aren't married).
- Why can't you be more like your brother or sister? (Implying that we must be inferior because we don't share the same skill-set.)
- I guess you're not as smart as I thought you were (implying they are disappointed in you.)
- You are very attractive for a heavy person (which part of that statement do you focus on?)

There are lots of ways in which our words can hurt other people and begin to cause rot and decay in their lives. Paul says we must avoid this kind of speech.

D. Martyn Lloyd-Jones looks at this unwholesome, or rotten, talk and points out three characteristics that are generally true of this kind of speech.

First, it flows out of excessive speech. It is possible for us to talk much but say little. The book of Proverbs declares, "When words are many, sin is not absent." (Proverbs 10:19) Sometimes we talk as a way to fill the silence while we think. We keep talking in the hopes that we will eventually stumble upon a point. When we aren't thinking about what we say, we are apt to say something that is rotten. We are in danger of unwholesome talk when we allow ourselves to blather on and on.

Second, it is self-serving. Though sometimes we need to talk about ourselves, we are in dangerous territory when we allow our speech to continually focus on us. Let's be honest, aren't there times when our primary purpose in talking is to make ourselves look good? Think about how we sometimes jump in to correct someone else or interject a story about ourselves. We are trying to show how smart or talented we are. In those situations, our speech is self-serving—our goal is to make ourselves look good with no thought of the other person.

When we engage in self-serving speech, we don't care what others have to say. People who commit this error often interrupt others. They interject and change the subject because they want to control the conversation and bring it back to themselves. You often see this mentality when you get a group of pastors together (I suspect it is the same way in many professions). Each person in the group is in a battle to prove how smart, successful, or spiritual they are. They want people to know the Lord is working in and through them...even if the church is small. The conversation is difficult to follow because every person jumps in to interject their own self-serving viewpoint. Over time, the volume level rises as everyone tries to talk over the group to be heard.

Even when we don't interrupt others, we can still be self-serving in our conversations. We don't pay attention to what someone is saying. When we tune someone out, we are communicating a message: "You are not important!" A pattern of self-serving talk is unwholesome and rotten.

Third, **unwholesome talk is indelicate.** Indelicate speech is brusque. We blast away without thinking about how the words will impact another. When we say things harshly, it is unwholesome. This kind of speech creates division in relationships, makes us look bad and is a terrible witness for the Kingdom.

If you're busy working on something and trying to concentrate, there are two approaches you can take with the person who is being a distraction. One is to tell them to "shut up!" That would be indelicate speech, and would be unwholesome. The other approach would be to consider that the other person didn't know they were being a distraction.

You could say, "I am in the middle of something here. Can you give me 5 minutes so I can give you my full attention?" There's a big difference between those approaches. One is concerned about how the other person will hear what we say; the other is only concerned about getting what we want.

We can also be indelicate when we say things that could be considered vulgar or offensive. When we speak in a vulgar or offensive manner, we are showing disdain for the people around us. Crass jokes, sexist comments, racial slurs, and more cause rot and decay.

The truth is we have all engaged in this kind of talk at one time or another. Here are some examples of unwholesome talk.

- Swearing/taking the Lord's name in vain
- Gossiping about others
- Using biting (or painful) sarcasm
- Making a joke at the expense of someone else
- Coarse/sexual talk or joking
- Violent talk

This is just a sampling of ways we can engage in unwholesome talk. Paul tells us that we should not allow this kind of talk to come out of our mouths. It may be the way the rest of the world talks, but as followers of Christ, we are called to be different. We should value each other enough to stay clear of words that wound.

What to Do Instead

Paul tells us not to let unwholesome talk come out of our mouths, and goes a step further and tells us what we should do instead. He says, "but [say] only what is helpful for building others up according to their needs, that it may benefit those who listen."

Paul says it's not enough just to avoid saying bad things, we should use our speech to build up others! John Piper sums up Paul's instruction nicely:

> *The issue is not whether our mouth can avoid gross language; the issue is whether our mouth is a means of grace. You see he shifts from the external fruit to*

the internal root. He shifts from what we say to why
we say it. That's the issue.[15]

Paul's concern isn't just that we avoid unwholesome talk, he tells us to change the entire motivation for *why* we talk. It is not enough for us to simply make ourselves sound clean; we must look for ways to make our words *benefit* others. Paul's instruction goes deeper than merely the words we say or the way we say them.

How Do We Do This?

How do we begin to develop the kind of speech habits that Paul says should be present in the life of a Christian? We cannot change our speech by mustering up enough willpower to do so. We can only change our speech by a change of heart. Jesus, when addressing the religious leaders, told them,

> *"Make a tree good and its fruit will be good, or make a tree bad and its fruit will be bad, for a tree is recognized by its fruit. You brood of vipers, how can you who are evil say anything good? For out of the overflow of the heart the mouth speaks." (Matthew 12:33-34)*

Jesus says what comes out of our mouths is a reflection of what is inside our hearts. What we say (especially in times when we are unguarded) reveals the true nature of what is inside of us. If we want to speak words that are beneficial to others, we need to start by working on what is inside of us.

There are several things we can do that will help us start making the change from being self-centered people with rotten speech to those who use our words to build up those around us.

First, choose to surround yourself with good influences. We tell our kids that they need to be careful in choosing their friends because their friends will rub off on them, but we often fail to take our own advice. If you surround yourself with unwholesome talk, it shouldn't surprise you when you begin to think (and talk) like the people around you! When we choose to be around people who tear down others or use vulgar language, we will begin to do the same things. When we watch

TV shows or movies, read web sites, or listen to music that is unwholesome, we are planting seeds within us that will start to grow rotting fruit.

In the book of Philippians, Paul gives us a better way,

> *Finally, brothers, whatever is true, whatever is noble, whatever is right, whatever is pure, whatever is lovely, whatever is admirable—if anything is excellent or praiseworthy—think about such things. (Philippians 4:8)*

If we want to be encouragers, **we should expose ourselves to others who encourage**. Listen to Christian music, hang around those who seem to exhibit this kind of speech, spend time reflecting on Scripture. We become like the influences we surround ourselves with— so we must choose those influences wisely. Pay attention to those people who encourage you. Learn all you can from them. Notice how they always seem to be looking for things to affirm (rather than criticize) in people.

Second, listen to yourself. Begin to pay attention to the things that you say. Let's face it, we often speak without thinking too much about what exactly we are saying. If you have children, you have probably had the same experience that I have: your children say something, and your immediate response is to scold them...until you realize they are simply repeating the things they have heard you say. Our children's speech patterns can act as a mirror to us to help us see the way we speak. But we shouldn't need our children to help us examine the things we say! I challenge you to start listening to the words you speak and the way you say them. Ask yourself a simple question—why did I say that? Look carefully at the motives behind why you say what you do, mindful of the fact that your words reveal what is in your heart.

Third, listen to others. I don't mean that we listen for all the ways other people mess up in their speech! What I mean is that we need to work at really paying attention to the way other people respond to what we say. Listen for the feedback others are giving you about your speech. When you say something, does the person snap back at you? If so, consider how what you said may have hurt them and caused them to lash out in anger. Learn to listen not just with your ears, but also with your eyes. Watch people's facial expressions as you speak (non-verbal communication is a huge part of conversation).

See how people wince when you say things that hurt, watch for them to break eye contact with you as though they are ashamed, look for the way their body language changes when you say things that build them up, and how it changes when you say things that wound their spirit. Watch for when people begin to lose interest (indicating you may have begun to ramble). And when you see a person beginning to make a fist...you would be wise to stop talking immediately!

Noticing the way people respond to what you say will help you be more sensitive to the needs of others. Suppose there is a person who has always been told they are dumb, or that they don't measure up. You may make a joke about something silly they have done, calling them a dummy or saying, "That wasn't very smart!" Those words carry more weight than you can imagine to that person. You don't intend to wound them, and if you aren't paying attention to the way they respond, you probably won't even realize that you did. The way others respond to our words can give us great insight into whether our speech is building them up or tearing them down. We can use this knowledge to adjust the way we speak.

Fourth, think about your thoughts. This is tough to grasp, but remember that everything we say starts as something we think. The Apostle Paul elsewhere tells us to take every thought captive and make it obedient to Christ. Examine the thoughts that run through your mind. Are they positive or negative? If you were to express those thoughts to someone else, would it build them up, or tear them down? We can exercise control over our tongues by exercising control over our thoughts. We can also choose what we are going to think about.

Craig Groeschel, in his book, *Soul Detox*, gives a really good principle to help us become better at encouraging and building up others. It's actually quite simple: *When you think something good about someone, say it*! Train yourself to build up others by working at actually telling them the good things you think about them. We live in a connected age, so this is not nearly as difficult as it would have been in some generations. As you think positive thoughts about another person, share those thoughts with them. You can do it in person, over the phone, in a letter, via text message, in an e-mail, on a Facebook post, or pretty much any way you can think of. The key is to begin expressing those positive thoughts. You will find that you become more aware of them the more you express them.

Lastly, enlist the help of a trusted friend. It is a difficult thing to examine our own speech. Your friends are probably more aware of your speech patterns than you are. Find someone you trust, who knows you well, and who has your best interests at heart and ask them to help hold you accountable. Give them permission to point out the times when you are being uncaring or hurtful in your words. This is a difficult thing to do, but having a friend who can "shoot straight" with you can help you to be honest with yourself about the things you say.

Conclusion

The task of changing our speech from rotten to beneficial is daunting. We are often unaware of all the things we say throughout the course of a day. If you're looking for a starting place, here's my recommendation: start by working on the way you talk to your family. We are most unguarded in our speech when we are around those with whom we are most comfortable. Look at the way you talk to your spouse, your children, your parents, or your siblings. Become aware of how your words affect those you love, and work at rooting out rotten speech in your home. If we can begin to change the way we talk at home, we will begin to see a significant change in the way we talk elsewhere.

Words are powerful! They have the power to wound or to heal. They have the power to tear down or to build up. They have the power to rot or to nourish. If we will strive to apply these principles in the way we talk to each other, we will see a change. People will be drawn to our churches as places where people really care. Christians will be people that others love to be around because they feel uplifted. People will see the love of Christ simply by spending time in conversation with us. As you guard your conversation, you will see people start to flourish and grow. And what's more, you will flourish and grow as well. Learning to speak like this requires hard work, but the payoff makes it worth the effort. The best time to get started is right now.

Dig Deeper

1. What is the most painful thing someone has ever said to you? What are some words you wish you could take back?
2. Enumerate ways to tell whether the people around you are having a positive or negative impact.
3. What is the difference between flattery and encouragement?
4. What kinds of things can we learn from nonverbal communication? What are some cues and what do they tell us?
5. Which suggestion in the chapter do you think will be most helpful to you?

Bruce and Rick Goettsche

9
Motivation for Godly Living
Ephesians 4:30

People are motivated by different things. It could be: money, love, fear, power, fame, or simply a modest goal they've set. This is also true for following Christ. Some are motivated by fear. They are afraid that if they do not do the right things, God will "get" them (kind of like Santa Claus with a naughty and nice list). Others believe doing Christian things will earn points that we can cash in when we need it later for blessings (kind of like turning in your tickets for a prize at a carnival).

Some strive to follow Christ because they believe in so doing they can make the world a better place. They believe Jesus was great with people (and they are right!) Others strive to live a "godly life" so they can fit in with their group of Christian friends. They know "Christians don't do certain things" (like cuss, lie, cheat, or hang out with certain kinds of people) so they try not to do those things (at least around those Christian friends).

In Ephesians 4:30 Paul gives us the best motivation for godly living,

And do not grieve the Holy Spirit of God, with whom you were sealed for the day of redemption. (Ephesians 4:30)

We must be careful with this verse. We need to grasp the tone of what is being said. It is easy to conclude that Paul is trying to guilt us into following the Lord. It's a trick that parents use all the time. "If you don't behave I will die and you'll be sent to an orphanage." Or you may hear it like a school administrator who says, "Behave yourself or we will call your parents."

I hope to show you that is not what Paul is trying to communicate. Paul wants us to understand that the Lord is deeply committed to us. His love is not distant, it is personal. God's Spirit lives inside of us. What we do and where we go, He goes with us. That partnership is a powerful motivation for pursuing the life of holiness.

What does it mean to Grieve the Spirit?

We have to think carefully about the answer to the question: in what sense does God grieve? God is not emotional in the same way we are. He does not respond emotionally to circumstances or to people. God does not make decisions because of emotions. He does not do things in reaction to other things. *Our* emotions are fickle. They are often tainted by sinful desires and thoughts. God always does what is right and what is true regardless of the situation. So God is not emotion-al in the same sense that we are.

However, this does not mean that God is emotion-less! Paul tells us that God does feel. God loves us passionately. It brings pain to the Spirit of God when we do not follow the right and true path that God has set before us. It pains Him to see us hurting ourselves or hurting others.

Perhaps the best way to understand this passion is to think about it in terms of parents and their children. As a parent you grieve when you see your child heading down a wrong path. You grieve when they ignore advice, make poor choices, and even when they have to live with the consequences that come because of their poor choices.

This is similar to how God feels about us. He wants what is best for us. He wants us to know His joy. He wants to guide us in a path that will allow us to experience His blessing and His love most fully. When we turn from that path He aches FOR us.

The Message, a Bible paraphrase (which means it is a very "free" translation) captures the essence of this verse well,

> *Don't grieve God. Don't break his heart. His Holy Spirit, moving and breathing in you, is the most intimate part of your life, making you fit for himself. Don't take such a gift for granted.*

Paul says we should strive to live holy lives because we have a *real* relationship with God. He is not simply "out there somewhere," He is close, personal, and vital in our lives. We know God's heart! He wants to bless us, not make us miserable. He wants to lead us out of the darkness of sin and into life as it was meant to be.

God cares! He is not like an unfeeling employer who is only concerned about the bottom line. He is not like the "friend" who only likes you when you do what they want. He cares about us as individuals.

Love is a powerful motivator. You will never forget the person who risked their life to save you (by donating an organ, rescuing you on the battlefield, pulling you out of a burning building, or maybe even standing at your side when the "whole world" was against you). When someone has stood by you through everything, you want to show them love in return.

The Lord made us. He came to rescue us in the person of Christ. He gave us His Word as a roadmap for life. He remains faithful when everyone else turns away. He sees the best in us even when we cannot see it in ourselves. This love, this relationship, should be the motivation for our new way of living. Our desire to walk with Him in fullest harmony should spur our diligence in eliminating all ungodly behavior.

In What Ways Do We Grieve the Spirit?

Paul has been giving us a list of some of the ways we can grieve the Spirit:

- When we are not unified as His body (v. 13)
- When we fall into error (v. 14)
- When we lie (vv. 15, 25) or don't speak to each other in love
- When we live only for the moment (v. 19)
- When we let anger consume us and make us mean (v. 26)
- When we steal or take what we have not worked for and become a burden on society and each other instead of contributing. (v. 27)
- When we tear others down instead of building them up. (vv. 28-29)

Paul is not finished with his list. It continues through the rest of the book. We will see that we grieve the Spirit when we…

- Lack gratitude and appreciation for God's gifts
- When we fail to extend forgiveness as we have been forgiven

- When we use each other instead of serve each other (especially in family relationships)
- When we fight supernatural battles in our strength rather than in his.

It is not only our behavior that grieves the Spirit. *We grieve the Spirit when we ignore Him in our lives.* Think about it, is anything more cutting than to be treated as if you don't exist or don't matter? Think about the hurt when someone refuses to have a relationship with you. They don't take your calls, they refuse to speak when they see you, and they won't even look you in the eye. They treat you as if you did not exist. You may want to be close to that person but they ignore you. Their actions (or inactions) break your heart.

When we ignore the directions God gives us, when we stray from the whispers of the Spirit that we often hear in our conscience, we are ignoring the Holy Spirit in the same way. When we neglect times of prayer or make it into a superficial exercise, we are treating Him as if He doesn't matter. When we ignore attentive Bible reading or merely view it as an academic exercise, we are effectively shutting our ears to God's instruction. This grieves the Spirit.

The *Holy Spirit also grieves when we are only interested in what God can give us rather than in who He is.* Think about how you feel when someone uses you. They pretend to be your friend when they want something, and when they get it, they act like they don't know you. They tell you how much they love you and need you until you give them what they want; then they grow tired of you. They try to learn everything they can from you until they get a promotion and then they treat you like you know nothing.

The phrase "Foxhole Christian" describes this kind "believer". They find themselves in some kind of crisis (such as a fierce battle in war) and are afraid they will not survive. In their fear they promise all kinds of things to God if He will only "get them out of" the situation. Then when the crisis passes, the promises are forgotten.

I see this all the time in the church. Someone starts attending church during a crisis because they know they need God's help. When the crisis passes, their seat in church is vacated.

When we only seek God in times of crisis, we show we are seeking His benefits rather than Him personally. We are using Him for our own selfish purposes. This grieves the Spirit because He wants a *relationship* with us.

Third the Spirit grieves when we refuse to respond to His Word or His promptings. God has given us the Bible and the Spirit to protect, enrich, and fulfill us. When we ignore them we show that we don't really trust Him. He has pointed out the way of life, and we have rejected it. Like a parent who grieves when a child spurns wise counsel, so God grieves for those who ignore His leading. (Those are the same people who often blame God when things go bad).

This is why the Holy Spirit grieves when we are absent from worship because He has given us the church to encourage and strengthen us in the battle of life. He has given us a day for rest and worship because He knows we need this to grow in our relationship with Him. Our absence is essentially refusing the means for growth and assistance that He has provided.

Fourth, *we grieve the Spirit of God when we fail to understand the goal of our salvation.* God wants to give us true life. He wants us to know the truth so it can set us free. He wants to prepare us for Heaven. He wants to build depth in us. But much of the time all we want is present relief and temporal treasures. We crave trinkets while God wants us to know a deep and abiding relationship with Him that transcends circumstances.

When we grieve the Spirit we put a strain on the relationship just like hurtful words strain a marriage relationship. When we push someone away long enough a barrier is erected. The same thing happens with the Holy Spirit. Every time we grieve the Spirit we put another brick in a wall that stands between us. This wall causes us to miss out on the fellowship and guidance He longs to give.

How Do We Guard Against Grieving the Spirit?

How do we keep from grieving the Holy Spirit of God? *First, we must remember God is committed to us.* Paul tells us that we have been sealed by the Spirit for the day of redemption. In other words, God is committed to save those who have put their trust in Him. Even though our commitment may be fickle, the Holy Spirit is committed to us. It is important to remember that our relationship with the Spirit is not an adversarial relationship. It need not be a struggle for power. It is a relationship of love. The directives of the Lord are anchored in love. We should serve Him out of delight rather than compulsion.

Just as remembering your wedding vows will help you to resist temptation to sin against your spouse; so remembering our commitment to Christ (and His commitment to us) will help us to resist the things that bring grief to the Spirit. It is good to wake up every day and remind yourself that you have been "bought with a price" and because of that fact you are a "new creation." This reality should motivate us to live in cooperation with His Spirit.

Second, *we must deal with that which grieves the Spirit immediately.* As in any relationship, when wrong is allowed to take root it becomes much harder to overcome. The same is true in our relationship with God. The more we try to hide, justify, and rationalize the wrong, the more invested we become in the lie.

We *are* going to stumble. The Lord is not surprised by our failures. The challenge is to restore fellowship as quickly as possible. We do that by admitting our sin, asking for forgiveness, and then turning in repentance and walking in His way.

Finally, we must *remember God's vision for our lives.* Many companies and churches emphasize the importance of a vision statement to remind people of what they are about and where they are going. In much the same way we must constantly remind ourselves that God desires a relationship with us that will last through eternity. God's desire is not merely for us to escape Hell, or have a more pleasant life; He wants us to become an active member of His household. He is not concerned about making us "comfortable." God is concerned about making us holy. God is concerned about our character. The Lord is less concerned about our status on earth and more concerned about our fitness for eternity. We must see the bigger picture and live in light of that picture.

Conclusion

So why is all of this important to us? *First, it impacts our focus for living.* Suppose someone asked: What is it like to be a parent? You could say "Being a parent is about battles to be fought, diapers to change, and vomit to clean up. It means you will feel that you are never going to be able to find any financial breathing room because there will always be something your child needs or wants. You will seldom know peace and almost never get to watch what you want on television. Parenting is one battle after another."

Are you drawn to the joy of parenting by these words? Of course not. Do you think such a person would be a good parent? It is not likely.

However, let's say the same question is asked of another person. They answer: "Parenting is a blessing beyond description. You will discover a capacity to love you didn't know you had. You will be extended a love you do not deserve. You get to not only watch someone grow but you get to help them as they do so. You will share in their joys and walk with them through the struggles. You will experience incredible pride at each new milestone when it is reached. It is a bond that is unlike any other. Parenting isn't always easy, but it is worth whatever effort is necessary."

What is your response to this person? This person makes you want to become a parent. They make you want to be part of such wonderful things.

Let's apply this to our walk with Christ. We can focus on the "burden" of sin, or the "sacrifice" of discipleship, or even the "struggle" against the enemy. Or we can focus on the "wonder of God's grace", the "privilege of sonship", and the "anticipation" of an inheritance that will not rust, fade, or spoil. We can strive to serve Him out of duty or we can serve because of the cherished nature of the relationship. Focusing on relationship, rather than burden, will motivate us much more effectively. It will also serve as a magnet which will draw others to the Savior's love. Paul is warning us to work hard for the right reasons.

Second, it reminds us that what we do and how we do it impacts more than just us. We live in a pretty selfish time. You hear people say, "I have to take care of my needs. I have to do what is best for ME." Of course, such statements assume that we actually know what is best for us (we don't). Selfishness not only grieves the Spirit – it also robs us of life and blessing.

Do you remember that day when you held your first child in your arms? At that moment your life took on a wider significance. It was no longer just about you. You realized that your actions now will impact your child either positively or negatively.

This is often the time when a couple will make out a will, buy life insurance, start saving money, and may even start to attend church because they want their children to grow up knowing God's leading and blessing. There are some who have spent their lives partying hard who now give up that lifestyle completely because there is so much at stake. They understand that they are no longer children, they are now responsible for the lives of others and that changes everything.

When we become a follower of Christ a similar thing should happen. We now belong to the royal family. We are children of the King of Kings and Lord of Lords. Our privilege and honor should change the way we approach life. This relationship should impact everything because it is so precious to us.

Serving the Lord is not about "keeping God from getting mad at us." It is not even about doing what we "should do." Paul urges us to serve the Lord and follow His commands because we are so loved by God that we want to demonstrate to Him that we love Him in return. It is a privilege, not a duty.

Dig Deeper

1. Did the love of your parents motivate you to live in a way that honored them? If so, how? In what ways did you grieve your parents?
2. How is absenting ourselves from the family of God in worship like skipping a family gathering?
3. How does our approach to Scripture and prayer either delight or grieve the Spirit?
4. What is your greatest motivation for holiness and for walking with the Holy Spirit?
5. If you were the Holy Spirit, what would grieve you about the lives of believers today?

10
A Better Way to Live
Ephesians 4:31-32

The Apostle Paul is giving examples of what it looks like to put off the old self and put on a new self so we can walk with Christ. He wants us to see clearly the life God created us to live. Paul has been specific and to the point.

Once again, we must remember that Paul is not telling us that we must do these things in order to *earn* salvation. Paul is arguing that these things are the *result* of our salvation. This is the goal of the Holy Spirit in our lives. If we are not making progress in these areas it is a sign that there is a problem in our spiritual lives.

In this chapter we look at the powerful verses in Ephesians 4:31-32.

Get rid of all bitterness, rage and anger, brawling and slander, along with every form of malice. Be kind and compassionate to one another, forgiving each other, just as in Christ God forgave you.

Paul builds on things he has already mentioned (anger and our conversation). The words are pointed and practical. Once again, Paul gives us negative behaviors we need to abandon and the positive behaviors to develop.

What to Stop
Bitterness. The first thing we are to work on eliminating from our lives is bitterness. Bitterness is a sour attitude that seeps into every area of our lives.

Bitterness happens most of the time because we fixate on hurts and replay them over and over in our minds. The hurts may be real or imaginary. We examine the hurt from every angle. We examine each word and tend to give it much more meaning than it ever could have had to start with. Bitterness feeds on itself and leads us to see hurts and grievances everywhere (even where they actually don't exist).

Bitterness and resentment are very human responses to pain but they are sinful responses. Rather than focus on hurts, it is better to focus on blessings and God's grace. The more aware we are of what we have been forgiven the more "unoffendable" we will become.

Next Paul tells us to get rid of **Rage and Anger.** The two words are related. Some have suggested that this is the result or outworking of bitterness. The word for rage or wrath is also translated by words such as passion and fury. It is an intense kind of anger that is dangerous. This is what happens to people who "lose their temper." Such people (at least temporarily) are "out of control." They are dangerous and can sometimes do great damage (physically or verbally) to others when they are in this state. An enraged person is one from whom you need to keep your distance. We need to take steps to never be that person who loses control.

The word Anger describes a more settled state. This is the person who is in a "bad mood." They pick at everything because they view everything from a negative perspective. An angry person can quickly turn into a person who moves to rage. Generally, however, rage is a temporary explosion. Anger is an attitude that lingers.

Next Paul says we should get rid of **Brawling and Slander.** This seems to be the verbal results of bitterness, wrath and anger.

Brawling is loud. You see this when people are shouting at each other in anger. We have all witnessed this kind of explosion and have been very uncomfortable because of it. It has happened to most of us at one time or another.

Brawling is unproductive. Nothing gets solved because no one is listening. It is often accompanied by crying and intense emotion. In these times, our words are usually sharpened and meant to wound. The goal of the brawler is not to reach a point of understanding and cooperation, the goal is to win, intimidate, or punish.

Here is a general principle: if you are raising your voice, you are probably sinning. Christians are to pursue peace. The tone and volume of our voice will inhibit productive relationships.

Slander is more devious. It is repeating things that are designed to make someone look bad or destroy a reputation. It operates in half-truths, exaggeration, and distortion. The word for slander is actually the word "blaspheme." We generally think of blasphemy as something (or someone) which slanders, misrepresents, or dishonors the character of God. Paul is giving this word an even wider usage. When we slander each other; when we diminish another person, we are actually slandering the Lord who made that person!

That's not really hard to understand. If someone makes fun or slanders your child, do you take it personally? Of course you do! God takes it personally when we slander others.

Every form of Malice. Paul leaves us no loop holes. Any behavior that destroys relationships or diminishes another person is to be eliminated from our lives. These behaviors are selfish and inconsistent with the Holy Spirit who has taken up residence in our heart. When we live this way, we grieve the Holy Spirit.

A.W. Tozer made a chilling observation.

> *We have all noticed how quick many people are to excuse themselves for some outburst by pleading that they were provoked to it. Thus their own wrongdoing is laid to others. What is overlooked in this neat trick of self-exoneration is that provocation cannot stir up what is not there. It never adds anything to the human heart; it merely brings out what is already present. It does not change the character; it simply reveals it.*
>
> *What a man does under provocation is what he is. The mud must be at the bottom of the pool or it cannot be stirred up. You cannot spoil pure water. Provocation does not create the moral muck; it brings it to the surface....*[16]

The point is simple: how we respond to each other (especially in times of conflict and tension) reveals more about our hearts than we may be ready to see.

The Better Way

Paul never leaves us without a solution. The believer in Christ can go in another direction because we have God's Spirit at work in us. We can leave this way of life behind! Paul gives us a formula for living that is pure, good, and powerful. If we do these things we will enjoy life, have friends, and influence many for the Kingdom.

> *Be kind and compassionate to one another, forgiving each other, just as in Christ God forgave you (Ephesians 4:32)*

Kindness is a goodness of heart. It is acting toward another person with consideration. The kind person acts in the best interest of the other person. The Bible tells us that love is kind. Kindness often begins with simple civility.

It involves seeing beyond ourselves so that we consider the needs of others or how our actions will affect those around us. For example, the kind person lowers their voice when they know someone is sleeping. They clean up a mess they made. They help out.

Kindness gives another the benefit of the doubt rather than assume the worst. Rather than jumping to a "worst case scenario," the kind person leaves the door open to the possibility of mitigating circumstances.

We are kind when we choose to spotlight strengths rather than weaknesses. We all appreciate it when someone spotlights the good things we do. We already have plenty of people who point out our faults.

Kind people refuse to be part of hurtful gossip.

Kind people will let someone else have the "spotlight." In other words it is letting someone have their "moment" without feeling like you have to "trump" their experience or turn the spotlight back to yourself. It is letting someone tell their story without feeling the need to jump in and correct them.

Sometimes being kind is simply listening to another who needs to talk.

One of the indicators of a depraved society is when people only care about themselves. If you look around you will see that kindness, respect and civility are becoming the exception rather than the rule. That is never good for a society. Rather than respond to people by being abrasive in return to their abrasiveness, the Bible teaches kindness as the antidote to the self-centeredness around us.

Compassion or tender-heartedness. The word used here is derived from a root word that means bowels. The idea is a compassionate person feels for someone from the depth of their being. They weep with those who weep and rejoice with those who rejoice.

The compassionate person is the one who learns to "put themselves in the shoes of another." For example, they will sense

- the fear, anxiety, and weariness of the person who is sick.
- the feeling of inadequacy in the one who is unable to provide for the needs of their family.
- the regret, embarrassment, isolation, and shame of the one who has failed and had it reported on the front page of the paper.
- the sense of hurt and rejection in the one who has been divorced.
- the loneliness and sense of isolation of the new student, employee, or church visitor.
- the fear of failure in the one who is reaching beyond their comfort zone.
- the desire for approval and attention in the child who won't stop talking.

We appreciate it when someone takes the time to truly understand us. At times, we have all felt like we were unseen, and because we are unseen, we quickly conclude that we don't matter. The compassionate person is the person who conveys the sense that someone DOES matter.

Forgiving. This last word is perhaps the most difficult. The word forgive comes from the root word of grace. To forgive means to "extend grace." The antidote to anger, resentment, bitterness, and aggressiveness is forgiveness.

Sometimes forgiveness means simply overlooking an offense. We all have bad days. We say things before we think. We make mistakes. Some things we should just overlook as just a part of being human.

However, some wounds are deeper. In this case forgiveness doesn't mean that we pretend it didn't happen. It is not about ignoring a wrong.

Forgiveness sees the wrong, recognizes the hurt or the injustice, and then chooses to extend grace rather than exact retribution. In other words, we choose to "let it go."

Three of my favorite words in Scripture come from one Greek word: Tetelestai, in English it is translated: "It is Finished." The guilt was dealt with once and for all on the cross. Jesus did not say, "It is begun" or "It is almost there." No...He said "it is FINISHED."

It is not that God has forgotten what we did...He chooses to "not remember." In other words, He considers the sin or offense no longer an issue in our relationship.

To forgive means we stop recalling and re-living the hurt. We give it to the Lord and move on. Forgiveness allows us to move forward rather than be tied to the past.

Pastor John Ortberg wrote,

Don't forgive, and your anger will be your burden.

Don't forgive, and bit by bit all the joy will be choked out of you.

Don't forgive, and you will be unable to trust anybody, ever again.

Don't forgive, and the bitterness will crowd the compassion out of your heart slowly, utterly forever.

Don't forgive, and that little grudge you nurse will grow larger, and stronger.[17]

Is forgiveness difficult? Of course it is! If you have ever been hurt deeply, you have struggled with forgiveness. We must struggle to forgive because God commands it and because a person who is unwilling to forgive is a person who invites bitterness, wrath, and anger into their lives.

Before we can forgive, we have to stop trying to vindicate ourselves and clear our name. We have to trust God to know the truth and vindicate us. If we do this, we will stop endlessly bringing up the hurt. (If you keep reminding someone (like your spouse) of a failure...you have not forgiven.)

We have all kinds of reasons why we think we think we should not, cannot, or will not, forgive. Most of these reasons boil down to just two: the depth of the hurt and the feeling that by forgiving justice will be perverted. Let's think about these.

First, there is *the depth of the hurt*. Let's concede that great hurt was done. It may have been physical, sexual, or psychological abuse. It may have been public disgrace, embarrassment, false charges, betrayal, financial loss, or shattered dreams. These are not little things. The Bible does not minimize our hurt. God does not make light of our sorrows.

However, we must keep perspective. We must remember that we have been forgiven by God. We have rebelled against His leadership, we have slandered His name, we have violated His laws, and we have treated Him as if He were nothing. We must ask a simple question: Has any hurt we have endured been as great as the assault that we have made against the God of creation? If we understand the cosmic ripple effect of sin we will realize that our sin makes even the most horrible actions of others seem minor by comparison…yet God forgives us through Christ. So, forgiveness is possible.

Second, there is *the issue of justice*. There is a feeling that if we truly forgive then the other person is going to "get away" with the wrong they have done. They will likely do it again. We feel the wrong demands some kind of payment.

Again, we have to ask ourselves if we are willing for that same standard to be applied to us? Paul asks: was not the crucifixion of Christ a sufficient punishment for sin? Was not the wrath that He endured in our place sufficient to pay for the sin of those who have offended us?

The Lord told us: "vengeance is mine, I will repay." Only God knows all the facts. He is the only one who knows the actions, motives, and mitigating circumstances of every situation. Our viewpoint is distorted. If more punishment is needed, the Lord is the one to hand it out…not us.

You are probably familiar with the texts in the Bible that tell us that if we have truly understood the forgiveness we have been given, we will likewise forgive others. In other words, Paul (along with Jesus) seems to be saying that in some respects forgiveness is a test of faith. If we are unwilling to forgive, it is possible that we have not understood what it is that we have been forgiven. It's possible that we aren't really believers at all!

Admittedly, these are strong words. God chooses His words carefully. The words are strong because this is apparently an important issue. Forgiveness matters!

Are you one who needs to do what Paul is telling us to do? Are you enslaved to bitterness and anger because you are unwilling to forgive? Are you playing some hurt over and over in your mind? Are you telling everyone you see that you have been treated shamefully? Do you relish opportunities to pass on information that will make the other person look bad? If so, you are not living with the heart of Christ.

Let me give you some specific suggestions on how to let go of the bitterness and embrace the heart of God.

1. Be honest with God. You may be able to fool yourself; you may be able to fool others; but you aren't fooling the Lord. God sees the churning, He hears the angry thoughts. He knows the malice you hide in your heart. Be honest with Him. Confess your hurt. Ask for Him to change your heart. Ask Him to help you to rest in Him.

2. Consider the grace that has been extended to you. Think about what you "deserve" and about what you have been given. Think long and hard. As you do, your heart will begin to soften.

3. Pray for the person who hurt you. At first you will be tempted to pray a simple prayer: "Get them God!" But that is not the prayer He desires. Bring that person to the Lord with the understanding that their behavior was an expression of a sinful and lost heart. See the danger they face. Then pray that God would open their eyes to His love, mercy and grace. Think about the things that may be motivating their behavior and bring that to the Lord. As we said a few chapters back, most anger is caused by some kind of pain in the angry person's life. Look for the pain and bring it before the Lord for healing. It is tough to stay angry and bitter if you are sincerely praying for someone.

4. DECIDE to forgive. You may need to do this every time you think about the offense and every time you begin to churn. In those times, choose to release the hurt and the one who hurt you

to the Lord once again. Declare it to be finished. You may need to do this for a long time, but don't give up. Decide to forgive over and over until (even though you remember the offense) it no longer impacts who you are and what you do.

5. Act in a forgiving way. This doesn't mean you have to hang out together. Work to be civil. Say hello. Shake their hand. Ask about the person's life. Act like the issue no longer matters between the two of you (even if you are you are still churning a bit about it). Try to work up to being kind. Remind yourself that this is less about them and more about you. What kind of person do you want to be? Are you willing to be God's agent even to those who have hurt you?

When you really struggle, ask yourself a simple question: Would I want God to treat me this way? Remember the grace that has been extended to you. Give thanks. Gain perspective. Pass that grace on to others.

If you will work at forgiveness, sometimes you will forget (most of the time you will *not* forget...what happened will simply become a "non-issue.") You will get past the hurt. You will see that we all need God's grace and we need to receive grace from each other. When we extend forgiveness, we experience that grace again in our own lives. We discover the freedom and the joy of entrusting our hurt to the Lord of life.

We can't do any of this in our own strength. We need the help of God's Spirit. Because of God's forgiveness, the chains of sin have been loosed in our lives. We have been given freedom and new life. At times it is hard to believe it's really true. How could God ever love us, after all we have done? But He does.

Having been given such freedom from our sin, why would we once again put on the straightjacket of bitterness, resentment, anger, and unforgiveness? Why choose to return to the prison from which we have been delivered? But that is exactly what we do when we choose not to forgive.

The Lord has set you free. Not only that, He has given us the opportunity, the privilege, and the joy, to extend that same wonderful grace, freedom, and forgiveness to others.

In these instructions Paul has challenged us to live in a way radically different from the rest of the world around us. He calls us to be kind, compassionate, tender-hearted, and forgiving. These seem to be endangered resources in our contemporary world. These things will not come naturally. They can only come through a supernatural work of the Spirit of God.

It may not be the easy way...but it is certainly the best way to live.

Dig Deeper

1. Which of these commands do you think is the most difficult? Why?
2. What are some of the effects from bitterness, resentment, malice, slander and other things have you witnessed?
3. Do you agree that these traits are endangered resources?
4. What are some false teachings or assumptions about forgiveness (e.g. you must forgive and forget) that hinder our ability to forgive?

11
Learning by Imitation
Ephesians 5:1-3

Paul argues: if we are true followers of Christ then our lives should begin to resemble the life of Jesus. The world should be able to see the character and demeanor of Jesus in the way we live our lives. They should see we walk with Jesus.

This should stand out in the way we define truth, deal with those who oppose us, conduct business, and make moral choices. People should see Jesus in the way we interact with the hurting and discarded. They should see it in our humility and desire to serve. They should see it in our homes and the way we honor, serve, and love each other.

At the beginning of Ephesians chapter 5 Paul states this difference with these words,

> *Be imitators of God, therefore, as dearly loved*
> *children and live a life of love, just as Christ loved us*
> *and gave himself up for us as a fragrant offering and*
> *sacrifice to God. (Ephesians 5:1-2)*

We are imitators of God when we do what Paul has been telling us to do. The word for imitate in the Greek is the word from which we get our word mimic. Think about someone who is really good at impersonations. They study their subject closely. They pay attention not only to what they say, but also the tone in which they say it, and the mannerisms of the person as they say it. The best impersonators sound and even look like the person they are imitating.

We Learn by Imitation

We are natural imitators. We learn to walk and talk by imitating (which is why people born in various parts of the country have distinctive accents). You can see imitation clearly in the young child going through various rituals in a batting box imitating their favorite hitter. We see it in the way we talk and the ideas which we hold. We even see this in the way we dress. Sometimes women will bring a picture of someone into the hair stylist and say, "I want to look like this."

We imitate those we admire. We adopt their vocabulary, we try to look like they look and behave as they behave. Sometimes this is unconscious. Paul challenges us to be conscious and deliberate about whom we are imitating.

In Romans 12:2 Paul wrote,

> *Don't copy the behavior and customs of this world, but let God transform you into a new person by changing the way you think. Then you will learn to know God's will for you, which is good and pleasing and perfect. (NLT)*

How Do You Imitate God?

The command to imitate God is a tall order. God is so different from us that this sounds like someone saying to us: "Imitate the Sun." How do you imitate a ball of fire?

Before we can imitate God we must understand that God has two kinds of attributes. There are attributes that are unique to God, called incommunicable attributes (or non-transferable) attributes. These attributes include God's eternal nature (God has existed for all eternity, we have not), His unchangeableness (we change all the time), or his characteristics as one who is all-knowing, all-powerful, and His ability to be present everywhere. We will never have these attributes. They belong only to God.

There are other attributes that we can imitate. These are called communicable attributes. We will never possess these things to the same degree God does, but they can become part of our lives and character. These attributes would include things like love, knowledge, mercy, wisdom, patience, justice and more.

We instinctively know those characteristics of God that are unreachable. Our challenge here is to be like God in the ways that we can be like God. The easiest way to do this is to imitate Jesus. Let me give you some Biblical examples.

We are to be like Christ in our generosity, as God has freely given to us so we should freely give.

> *But just as you excel in everything—in faith, in speech, in knowledge, in complete earnestness and in your love for us—see that you also excel in this grace of giving. (2 Corinthians 8:7)*

We are to be like Jesus in the way we respond to those who attack us.

> *To this you were called, because Christ suffered for you, leaving you an example, that you should follow in his steps. "He committed no sin, and no deceit was found in his mouth." When they hurled their insults at him, he did not retaliate; when he suffered, he made no threats. Instead, he entrusted himself to him who judges justly. (1 Peter 2:21-23)*

Since Jesus did not return evil for evil we should not do so either. Since He let God handle any injustice toward Him as a person, we should do likewise.

We are to be like Jesus in humility and service.

> *Do nothing out of selfish ambition or vain conceit, but in humility consider others better than yourselves. Each of you should look not only to your own interests, but also to the interests of others. (Philippians 2:3-4)*

Jesus wasn't concerned about what was best for Him. His concern was only what would please and honor His Father in Heaven. These are admittedly tough traits to imitate but we are to try to do so.

Imitating Love

In Ephesians 5:2 Paul focused on just one example of an attribute that we can imitate: love. It is a popular term but a difficult trait to practice. We use the word "love" quite freely today. We love sports teams, music groups, vehicles, electronic gadgets, books, movies, clothes, hairstyles, and various people (many of whom we don't even know). Love as defined by the world around us tends to be selfish. Its focus is feelings. We love those things which bring us some kind of pleasure. This is why people tell you that they "fell out of love" with someone. They mean by this that they no longer derive the same pleasure from someone or something.

Our challenge is to learn to love others not on the basis of how they make us feel, but because they are created by God and are therefore worthy of love. It is the kind of love that is consistent and is what we talk about when we promise to love for better or worse, richer and poorer, in sickness and in health. It is a love that reaches to people we like and even those we don't like. Jesus said,

> "You have heard that it was said, 'Love your neighbor and hate your enemy.' But I tell you: Love your enemies and pray for those who persecute you, that you may be sons of your Father in heaven. He causes his sun to rise on the evil and the good, and sends rain on the righteous and the unrighteous. If you love those who love you, what reward will you get? Are not even the tax collectors doing that? And if you greet only your brothers, what are you doing more than others? Do not even pagans do that? (Matthew 5:43-47)

Our Motivation

Every challenge needs a motivation. Every year a sports team goes through training camp motivated by the desire to be a champion. We are motivated by laws, by profit potential, or by a dream of doing something significant. Paul gives the motivation of all motivations when he said "live a life of love, just as Christ loved us and gave himself up for us as a fragrant offering and sacrifice to God." Our motivation for living a life after the pattern God has set is the love that we have received from God.

We see God's love illustrated quite graphically in the sacrificial death of Jesus. In Romans 5 we read this description,

When we were utterly helpless, Christ came at just the right time and died for us sinners. Now, most people would not be willing to die for an upright person, though someone might perhaps be willing to die for a person who is especially good. But God showed his great love for us by sending Christ to die for us while we were still sinners. And since we have been made right in God's sight by the blood of Christ, he will certainly save us from God's condemnation. (Romans 5:6-9, NLT)

Note, **God showed His love for us even though we were undeserving**. God also sent His Son knowing we would *continue* to be undeserving! The Bible is clear. We have all sinned and fall far short of the requirements necessary to be right with God. We are all guilty of what has been called "cosmic treason." We have ignored the reign of God and have made up our own rules. The reason the world is in the mess it is today is because we have *refused* to do what God has told us to do.

In spite of all this, God sent His Son to pay the price for our sin. He did this because of *His* love, not because of *our* goodness. As the old song says, "He looked beyond our fault and saw our need." If we are going to imitate God, then we must learn to look past the behavior or appearance of people to the image of God that is buried in the rubble of their life. We must see what God sees in others. We must see what God sees in us.

Second, **Jesus died willingly.** Jesus was not a victim of circumstances. He was not "in the wrong place at the wrong time." He *chose* to surrender His life as an atonement (or payment) for sin. One of the things you see clearly in the gospels is that Jesus knew why He had come to earth. He warned the disciples. He agonized in prayer. He surrendered to the Father's plan. He did all of this before He was ever arrested by the Jews.

Love is a choice. If we are going to imitate God, then we must love willingly, not because we have been forced to love. Coerced love is not genuine love. Our world sees love as an emotion. It believes we must "feel close" to or "be attracted" by a person before we can love them. God calls us to choose to love whether or not we "feel" like doing it.

Often feelings of love will come *after* we have decided to love. This is because we have determined to look for that which is loveable. This is just the opposite of what we normally do. Usually we are attracted by certain character traits and then push away because of the negative things we observe. And once we start focusing on the negative look out! We will see negatives everywhere. We need to turn things around. When we look at potential rather than failures people become much easier to love. And let's face it, isn't this what we want others to see in us?

Third, **Love is Costly**. The love of God cost Jesus His life. He suffered the penalty that we deserved. When Jesus hung on the cross, the pain of the crucifixion (e.g. the nails, abuse, and suffocation) was secondary to suffering the wrath of God. Since God is holy and just He must punish wrong behavior (otherwise it is a perversion of justice). He punished Jesus in our place. This is why Jesus cried out "My God, My God, why have you forsaken me?"

Let's say your child did something horribly wrong. For the purpose of the illustration imagine they were involved in reckless behavior that resulted in the death of someone. Your child goes to court and is convicted of 2nd degree murder and sentenced to 15 years in prison. No one doubts the sentence is fair and just.

Now suppose that you as the child's parent step forward and agree to serve the time for your son. The Judge agrees because the demands of the law would be satisfied. The sentence would be carried out and the crime would be punished. However, because of your action your son has a chance to do something positive with his life.

This is what God has done for us. Our offense was much worse and consequently the penalty much greater. However, Jesus took our place and suffered our penalty. He was our substitute. He is able to do this for so many people because as the Son of God. His life is of infinite worth. Jesus died so that we could know life.

Return to that boy and his father. What kind of impact do you think the Father's sacrifice would have on his son? It's possible the son might squander his opportunity to live a new life and view his father as a chump. But it is more likely that this son would be changed forever by the love of his Father. Every time he visited dad in prison, every time he thought about what his father had sacrificed for His freedom, he would be motivated to live differently. He would be much more loving because He witnessed love in the act of His father.

This is what Paul is telling us to do. We are to remember how God has loved us, to embrace that love, and then to allow it to change us forever. Love is not easy. In fact, love often brings pain. It is messy. Love takes time, it requires sacrifice and it means setting aside thoughts about what "we deserve." It is hard in marriage and in every other relationship of which we are part.

How Do We Proceed from Here?

What should we do in light of all of this? I have some suggestions.

First, **embrace this love of God for you**. The Bible summons us to entrust ourselves to this One who loves us with an everlasting love. It seems foolish to walk away from such love yet people do it every day! They hear the truth and simply don't care! They want to do their own thing. They take a pass on the love God wants to give.

It is impossible to love in the way we are challenged to love if we have not first experienced this love from the Father's hand. We are all tempted to try to EARN God's love, but there is no way to do this. Before we will ever be able to love, we have to first allow ourselves to know the love of God.

We are broken people. That fact does not change even when we come to Jesus. What changes is the fact that we are forgiven people. This forgiveness makes all the difference in the world. God has come to set us free from our past, present, and the future path to which we are heading. Why would you resist His offer of forgiveness and new life?

Are you ready but don't know what to do? You start by running to Him rather than turning from Him. It is about believing that His sacrifice is sufficient for your sin and resting in His forgiveness. Simply put, Have you ever said, "Yes" to Jesus?" Are you willing to let Him love you?

Max Lucado relates this account,

In one of Henri Nouwen's books, he tells about the lesson of trust he learned from a family of trapeze artists known as the Flying Rodleighs. He visited with them for a time after watching them fly through the air with elegant poise.

111

When he asked one of the flyers the secret of trapeze artists, the acrobat gave this reply:

The secret is that the flyer does nothing and the catcher does everything. When I fly to Joe [my catcher], I have simply to stretch out my arms and hands and wait for him to catch me and pull me safely over the apron....

The worst thing the flyer can do is to try to catch the catcher. I am not supposed to catch Joe. It's Joe's task to catch me. If I grabbed Joe's wrists, I might break them, or he might break mine, and that would be the end for both of us. A flyer must fly, and a catcher must catch, and the flyer must trust, with outstretched arms, that his catcher will be there for him.[18]

This is the picture of salvation: our job is to stretch out and trust that God is able to do what He says, and what He has proved He can do. We must stop trying to save ourselves and rest in the arms of Jesus.

Second, **Study the character of God.** It is impossible to imitate someone you do not know. It is impossible to imitate mannerisms of which you are unfamiliar. The same is true with the Lord. We must get to know Him. We do this through reading the Bible, through quiet reflection, and by talking with Him. Listen to what Jesus taught and learn from how He responded to others. Watch Him. Listen to what He said. Notice how differently He responded to people than we do. Begin to apply those lessons to your own life. You might even pick up a good book on the attributes of God and read it devotionally.

Third, **Make the effort to put into practice what you learn.** Let's go back to the toddler who is learning to walk. At first when the toddler tries to pull themselves up, it is frustrating. They only stand for an instant and then they fall. The whole process of learning to walk requires overcoming many frustrations and failures.

Let's suppose the child tried to get up and said to themselves, "This is too hard. I am sure I can't do this." Obviously the child would never learn to walk, run, or probably do anything else.

The same is true in our Christian life. Much of the time we know what we are supposed to do. The problem is that we are afraid to make the effort. We are concerned that we will mess things up or fail, or humiliate ourselves.

No matter what we set out to do in life we are not going to be very good at it at the beginning. We will stumble. We will fall. We will fail. And this will happen again and again and again. We will look pretty unbalanced and feel like we are out of our league. And this is where the choice comes in. We must make the effort.

We need to take one step at a time. This may involve having a conversation with a friend about their relationship with God; or changing some deeply ingrained habit in your life. It may necessitate radically adjusting your values. You will need to learn to look past the surface of people and see what God sees...the treasure. It is not enough to talk about doing these things...we need to make the effort. The biggest reason we fail to change is because we often fail to begin!

This isn't going to be easy. It will take practice and hard work to imitate His life.

- It is not easy to love someone who attacks you.
- It is not easy to serve someone who taunts you.
- It is not easy to remain pure in a world that regularly negotiates morality and purity.
- It is not easy to be humbly dependent in a world that applauds pride and arrogance.
- It is not easy to forgive someone who wounded you.
- It is not easy to fulfill commitments when those commitments are more costly than you anticipated.

None of these things are easy. However, we aren't asked to imitate God because it is easy. We are told to imitate Him because His way is the best way; it is the only way that leads to new life.

Let me warn you: you will fail at times. However, as you grow in the Lord those times of failure will be less often and less severe.

As we learn to imitate God, His power will be released in our lives. We will know greater joy and peace. We will view people with new eyes and learn to love more unselfishly.

As we imitate the Lord we will also reveal Him to the watching world. People need to see Jesus at work in our lives before they will ever believe what we have to say about Him. So, in that sense, imitating the Lord in the way we live really is a matter of life and death.

Dig Deeper

1. Who has been a model in your life? Who have you tried to imitate?
2. Why do people find it hard to believe someone who is not living a Christ-like life?
3. Try to illustrate the difference between the love of the world and the love of God.
4. Who are the people you find most difficult to love? Why?

12
Changing Our Diet
Ephesians 5:3-15

One of the things we learn (especially as we get older) is: if we want to stay healthy we need to watch what we eat (and I don't mean as it goes into our mouths). It is common to hear people are on diets that restrict salt, sugar, or other kinds of food because of health issues. It is a reality that a change in health doesn't come about without a change of behavior.

When my niece was diagnosed with juvenile diabetes as a young girl her whole family had to learn how to think about food in a whole new way. They had to learn how to do blood tests and how to calculate how much insulin was needed to balance whatever food intake there was. They had to live differently.

Even I am reluctantly learning that if you want to lose weight the same is true. I must stop eating things that are bad for me and begin to eat better. I also need to add more exercise to my life. I may not like this, but it is the truth.

These same things are true about being a follower of Christ. The apostle Paul has been talking to us about our spiritual diet. If we are going to imitate God it will require that we make some changes in the way we live.

It is tempting to hear these words in Ephesians 5:3-17 as negative and harsh and respond with resistance rather than openness as you would to someone who is trying to "tell you what to do." However, I encourage you to hear these words as the words of a Doctor who is trying to save your life. Paul writes,

> *But among you there must not be even a hint of sexual immorality, or of any kind of impurity, or of greed, because these are improper for God's holy people. Nor should there be obscenity, foolish talk or coarse joking, which are out of place, but rather*

thanksgiving. For of this you can be sure: No immoral, impure or greedy person—such a man is an idolater—has any inheritance in the kingdom of Christ and of God. Let no one deceive you with empty words, for because of such things God's wrath comes on those who are disobedient. Therefore do not be partners with them. (Ephesians 5:3-7)

What Needs to be Removed

Paul is speaking to believers. He is not trying to legislate morality for the general public. It is difficult for non-Christian people to embrace the standards listed here because they are coming from an entirely different perspective. In their minds the will of the majority is what determines morality. If the majority approved of polygamy (being married to multiple people) it would eventually be considered appropriate and laws might be written to that effect.

As believers, however, we determine our morality from the Law of God. Since God is Sovereign and perfect in wisdom, since He is the Creator and designer of life, we recognize that His commands are superior to our desires. We do not see clearly; He does. We don't see long term repercussions to choices; He does. We don't see the long-term impact on relationships, society, and our spiritual life; He does. We live differently from the rest of the world because we define truth differently. With that said, let's look at what Paul tells us to eliminate from our diet.

Sexual Immorality. The word used here is porneia (from which we get "pornography"). This word refers to an improper sexual relationship of any kind. Any sexual relationship outside of a marriage between a man and a woman is immoral (wrong or harmful) by God's standards. In a culture that says intimacy before marriage is "accepted practice," where sexual infidelity is frequent, and where laws legalize same sex unions, this seems extreme. However, when we turn to the Creator and designer, He tells us that any sexual intimacy outside of marriage cheapens this gift of God and impacts the individual and society in negative ways. It turns intimacy into something selfish (for our pleasure) instead of being an act of commitment and love.

You don't have to tell your non-Christian friends and neighbors how they should live their lives! Your job is to live the way God has called you to live. We are to live as a member of God's family.

Every family has rules. The members of the family must learn these rules to live in harmony with each other. The rules in different families are not all the same. The rules for the family of God are designed to help us live and function in a healthy way,

Any Kind of Impurity. This takes the issue of purity one step further. Immoral behavior is not just related to the act of sexual intimacy. It also includes "any kind of impurity." I believe this includes contemporary problems such as: pornography, sexting, suggestive comments (verbal or electronic with someone other than your spouse), a host of cyber behaviors, and anything else you can imagine. Paul shows that this is an area of life that is a battleground. It is a point of vulnerability against which we must guard ourselves. More and more we see marriage problems that are related to media abuses. It can be as simple as people constantly on their phones or texting, all the way to "cyber affairs." These sins undermine relationships and are an offense to a holy God. Can such sins bring pleasure? Of course they can! For a time. If sin was not pleasurable, it would hold no attraction.

Greed. Greed is the motivator behind much of the sexual immorality and impurity that we have just talked about. It stems from the desire to have what (or whom) we desire. Greed includes a preoccupation with money and "stuff" of any kind. The materialistic mindset puts trust in material things rather than the Lord! We start to believe that a new car, home, computer, cell phone, pair of jeans...will fulfill us and make us happy.

Greed may also manifest itself in a competitive spirit (this happens even among churches). It is the desire to be "better" than everyone else. This greed leads to a competitive spirit, the tendency to spotlight and magnify faults, and does sometimes irreparable damage to the body of Christ.

The Bible says anything in which we put our hope, or is more important to us than the Lord, is an idol! It has taken the place of God in our lives! Our churches can even become idols!

Obscenity. Obscenity includes but is more than just bad words. It is anything that is indecent or offensive. It is talk or actions that have no regard for proper standards of behavior. It is very close to blasphemy. In other words, obscenity is when we take God's name, character, or attributes and speak of them in a disrespectful way. Let me give you a couple of common examples: think of all the phrases that sometimes follow the word "Holy" (smoke, mackerel, cow). All of these diminish the exalted concept of God's holiness, purity, and excellence. The common OMG statements in texts, Facebook, and other places refer to God as if He were nothing, or at best commonplace. This is obscene.

You can add to this: suggestive comments, off-color jokes, and profanity of any kind. I have noticed that many entertainers could benefit from a Thesaurus because their vocabulary is very limited!

Foolish Talk. In Greek the word for "foolish talk" is "morologia" it is a combination of "moron" and "talking." It is to talk like a moron or a fool. It is when we make light of high standards of behavior and think it is funny or even sophisticated to make light of what is praiseworthy. As you look through the various verses in Proverbs there are several characteristics of foolish talk,

- Fools speak without thinking and it gets them into trouble (Proverbs 18:6-7)
- Fools slander others and they are quick to pass on gossip (Proverbs 10:18)
- Fools think wrong is funny and mock the commands of Scripture (Proverbs 14:9)
- Fools quarrel about everything (Proverbs 20:3)
- Fools speak nonsense; they just like to hear themselves talk (Proverbs 15:2)

Coarse Joking. The Bible is not against a sense of humor (God made us with a sense of humor). What is forbidden for the believer, is coarse or off-color humor. This would be when we make fun of others, joke about sin, or tell jokes that we probably would not (or should not) want to tell in front of our children, our mom, or more importantly, the Lord. If you feel that a certain joke would be inappropriate from the pulpit…it is humor you should eliminate.

What Makes These Things Bad?

On the surface of things it sounds like Paul is being pretty trivial. However, the reasons for giving attention to these things are sobering.

First, he tells us that these behaviors provoke the wrath of God. In other words, this is serious stuff. Paul says "because of such things God's wrath comes on those who are disobedient."

The wrath that comes reveals itself in at least two ways. *First, it will reveal itself on the Day of Judgment.* In 1 Corinthians 6 we read,

> *Don't you realize that those who do wrong will not inherit the Kingdom of God? Don't fool yourselves. Those who indulge in sexual sin, or who worship idols, or commit adultery, or are male prostitutes, or practice homosexuality, or are thieves, or greedy people, or drunkards, or are abusive, or cheat people—none of these will inherit the Kingdom of God. Some of you were once like that. But you were cleansed; you were made holy; you were made right with God by calling on the name of the Lord Jesus Christ and by the Spirit of our God. (1 Corinthians 6:9-11, NLT)*

Galatians 5 says much the same,

> *When you follow the desires of your sinful nature, the results are very clear: sexual immorality, impurity, lustful pleasures, idolatry, sorcery, hostility, quarreling, jealousy, outbursts of anger, selfish ambition, dissension, division, envy, drunkenness, wild parties, and other sins like these. Let me tell you again, as I have before, that anyone living that sort of life will not inherit the Kingdom of God. (Galatians 5:19-21, NLT)*

These are strong words! Paul says people who live like this will not go to Heaven...unless they repent! It does not matter what prevailing public opinion is! It does not even matter what the law of the land says. If we continue in these things...the Bible says we will not be saved.

This makes us very uncomfortable. I suspect we can all find something in this list of which we have been (or are) guilty. It is important to understand that Paul is not saying that such people can *never* be forgiven...the sacrifice of Christ makes it possible for us to be forgiven of each and every sin! In the 1 Corinthians passage Paul said that many who were in the church had come out of these very behaviors!

The key is that we must come out of this lifestyle! We are to "put away" these things. That doesn't mean we won't stumble, but when we do, we will immediately repent and seek God's strength to overcome the behavior that is offensive and leading us away from Him (and each other). In other words, if a person makes a profession of faith in Christ but their lifestyle doesn't change (though change often comes gradually)...it reveals that their profession of faith in Christ was false.

Is God being overly harsh? I don't think so. Think about it: God clearly told us what He expects, He provides us a Redeemer to pay for our sin, and He offers the Holy Spirit to make us new inside and to empower us to do what is right. I can't help but think that if we continue to treat God with contempt or indifference; if we continue to debase what He has called holy; if we refuse His offers of forgiveness and love; why would we be surprised at facing His wrath and judgment?

We also experience God's wrath in our day to day living. How? Part of God's present judgment is to let us live with the consequences of our choices. The scars we carry, the empty relationships we endure, the conflict we produce with our words, the fractured homes, the growing sexual perversions, the increase in violent behavior, and the sense that God is far away are all consequences of our refusal to follow the way of Christ. When we play with the fire of sin we will get burned!

From time to time people will ask, "Why does God allow all the evil and corruption in the world?" The answer is: God is giving us what we wanted. We are living with the consequences of our choices.

Second, Paul also gives us a positive motivation for obedience: Darkness has been replaced with Light.

> *For you were once darkness, but now you are light in the Lord. Live as children of light (for the fruit of the light consists in all goodness, righteousness and truth) and find out what pleases the Lord. Have nothing to do with the fruitless deeds of darkness, but rather expose them. For it is shameful even to mention what the disobedient do in secret. But everything exposed by the light becomes visible, for it is light that makes everything visible. This is why it is said:*
>
> *"Wake up, O sleeper,*
> *rise from the dead,*
> *and Christ will shine on you." (Ephesians 5:8-14)*

Don't miss the wording here. Paul does not say (v. 8) that we are living IN the light. He says we ARE the light. As His followers, we are to reveal His light to others. The best testimony we have is our life! If we continue to live like everyone else, we have surrendered to the enemy! We have turned off our light!

Paul instructs us to expose the deeds of darkness. This isn't about wagging our finger in someone's face and telling them they are going to Hell! We expose the darkness when we turn on the light! In other words, when we show honor to each other, when we maintain standards of purity even though people mock us, and when we guard our words so that we always speak with respect about the things God has called sacred, we show, by contrast, that the alternative is emptiness and darkness.

A Strategy for Success

Let's get practical. How can we pursue God's standards more effectively?

Show honor, respect, and gratitude for the things which God has given. Each of the things we are warned about is actually a perversion of a good gift of God for which we should be thankful.

Sexual intimacy is designed to bring a husband and wife together in a vulnerable and intimate way that draws them wonderfully close to each other and deepens their relationship. It is a way to give of oneself to another in love. The perversion of the gift is about selfishness and satisfying our desires. One exalts God, the other exalts pleasure. We should guard and be grateful for the good gift God has given.

The person who brags about all their sexual partners is really just telling everyone they are incapable of a committed relationship of love. They declare themselves to be users rather than lovers.

We should be grateful for material blessings and realize that everything we have belongs ultimately to the Lord. God cares for us and provides for us. He gives us the tools we need to help others and to be agents of His love. Instead of worshipping at the altar of the material, we should receive God's gifts with gratitude and use them for God's glory.

We should be grateful for the transforming nature of God's truth. Rather than making light of truth and distorting it with our flippancy, crude behavior, or complaints about God's "burdensome rules," we should show respect and honor for this truth that sets us free.

We should be grateful that words can be agents of healing, encouragement and grace. We can change people's lives with our words (good or bad). We can lift spirits, impart strength, and encourage confidence. We can also discourage, defeat, and embarrass others. With our words we can worship God in a way that draws us close to Him. Words are a special gift that we must cherish rather than defile by using them to destroy others and make light of the greatness of God.

We must do an honest inventory of our lives and weed out destructive habits and behaviors. To do this we need to monitor what we read, watch, and listen to. As I have said before, every program, song, book or movie is advancing some kind of value system. Think about the messages we receive from the media around us:

- Sex is recreational; it is about pleasure not intimacy. Sex before marriage is normal and a good way to "test" our potential mates.

- Adultery is often justified (think about the fact that we sometimes find ourselves in movies and TV shows "rooting" for the married person to get out of their "loveless" marriage to be with their "soulmate.")
- God is whatever we believe Him to be and truth changes with the individual.
- Value and significance is determined by what we look like, how much we earn, and what we own (or drive).
- A lie is determined by the situation not by any external standard of truth.
- Revenge is satisfying.
- The only true standard of behavior is that there is no standard of behavior. Everyone should be able to do what is right in their own eyes.

All of these things are lies from the pit of Hell! Constant exposure to sinful values will slowly erode us. If we view and listen to these things long enough we begin to conclude that these things are "acceptable practice" simply because everyone says so. We have to pay attention! Paul tells us to "Be very careful, then how you live—not as unwise but as wise, making the most of every opportunity because the days are evil." (vv. 15-16)

This whole lesson about changing our diet is summarized succinctly by this story.

> *An old Cherokee was telling his grandson about a fight that is going on inside each person. He said it is between two wolves. One is evil and is characterized by: anger, sorrow, regret, greed, arrogance, self-pity, guilt, resentment, inferiority, lies, false pride, superiority, and ego...*
>
> *The other is good and is characterized by: joy, peace, love, hope, serenity, humility, kindness, benevolence, empathy, generosity, truth, compassion, and faith.*

The old Cherokee again reiterated that the battle was fierce.

The grandson listened with rapt attention. He thought about it for a minute and then asked his grandfather, "Which wolf wins?"

The old Cherokee simply replied, "The one I feed."

The old Cherokee was a wise man.

Dig Deeper

1. Which of the things we are to remove from our lives will be the most difficult for you? Why?
2. These commands are for Christians. Why is it wrong to try to get non-Christian people to do these things? What happens when we do try to force others to live God's way? What should we be doing to help our friends and neighbors?
3. How does the love of Christ motivate us?
4. Can you add to the list of the messages shouted at us from the media and in the world in general?

13
Walking Carefully
Ephesians 5:15-17

In the military, combat engineers are sometimes tasked with the job of clearing a path through a minefield. Their job is to remove the mines in a given area so that troops can move safely. After they have cleared a path that is safe to travel through, troops and vehicles are allowed to move through the area.

As people travel through the zone, however, it is important to stay only in the area that has been cleared. In a minefield, there are clear markings that show where it is safe to walk. The person who stops paying attention to where they are could find themselves in grave danger.

In the last chapter, we looked at the kind of spiritual "diet" that we should have in our lives. Paul told us the kinds of behaviors that should be present and those that should be absent. He said since we have been brought into the light, we must live differently than those who walk in darkness. He continues that thought in verses 15-17, where he tells us that we should be very careful how we live, much as a person has to be careful when traversing a minefield.

> *Be very careful, then, how you live—not as unwise but as wise, making the most of every opportunity, because the days are evil. Therefore, do not be foolish, but understand what the Lord's will is. (Ephesians 5:15-17)*

Paul gives three instructions for how to carefully live out our lives.

Live Wisely
Paul's first instruction is to live wisely. The Bible talks a great deal about wisdom and contrasts it with foolishness.

The book of Proverbs is written as a way of passing on wisdom to the next generation. Proverbs declares there is nothing in the world that is more valuable than wisdom:

Wisdom is supreme; therefore get wisdom. Though it cost all you have, get understanding. (Proverbs 4:7)

Wisdom is of greater value than anything else in the world because it will give us success in life, and help us understand what true success really is. So, what is wisdom? It may be easier to define wisdom by pointing out what it is not.

Wisdom is not the same thing as knowledge. A wise person often has a great deal of knowledge, but having extensive knowledge does not guarantee that you are wise. Wisdom is the ability to apply the knowledge, experience, and skills you have to discern how best to proceed in a given situation—and then actually apply that wisdom to your life! There are many people who can explain all sorts of lofty concepts to you, yet seem to have no idea how to actually live their lives. They make poor choices and find their lives in shambles. These people have knowledge, but little wisdom.

A simple example of wisdom is the parent with a child who is resisting them. The child may be throwing a fit, seeking to make life miserable for their parent, hoping the parent will simply give in to their demands. A wise parent knows that there is more at stake than just whether the child gets what they want in this moment. Even if what the child is demanding is harmless, a wise parent will still deny the child's wishes because they see the bigger issue. They know that rewarding the child's bad behavior by giving them what they want will have disastrous consequences down the road. A wise parent is willing to endure the wrath of their child in the short-term, in order to teach their child character and right behavior in the long-term.

This is quite a contrast to the way the world today functions. We are encouraged to "follow our hearts" or to do what "feels right" or "live in the moment." This is the epitome of foolishness! The wise person recognizes that simply doing what "feels good" is not a good test for determining what is right. The wise understand following feelings and desires will often lead into a dangerous mine field.

If we only followed our desires, we wouldn't get out of bed in the morning to go to work, because we would rather sleep. If we did go to work, we would only do our jobs when we felt like it, because we desired to check Facebook, or do some online shopping, talk to our friends, or take a nap. If we only followed our desires, we would be dangerous with a credit card, because we would simply buy what looked attractive to us, even if we had no way to pay for it. And, we would be overweight and in poor health because we would eat poorly (lots of junk food). Our marriages would crumble because we would walk away from our spouse after a fight because we no longer "loved them."

Does this sound at all like our society? This is the result of living the way our culture says—being driven by our feelings and desires. Living this way is foolish and has disastrous consequences. You and I may not make all of these mistakes, but we do make some of them. When we choose to think only about our present desires without really weighing the consequences of our actions, we act foolishly.

The wise person is able to take a step back from the situation and see beyond this moment. Here is how James tells us we can recognize a wise person,

> *Who is wise and understanding among you? Let him show it by his good life, by deeds done in the humility that comes from wisdom. (James 3:13)*

Paul says that since we have been made new by God, we must be careful to live wisely instead of living foolishly. It is not enough to know the right way to go, we must choose to do it.

Make the Most of Every Opportunity

The second instruction Paul gives is in verse 16,

> *Making the most of every opportunity, because the days are evil. (Ephesians 5:16)*

Paul's instruction, translated literally, is "redeem the time." In other words, Paul wants us to see that time is a valuable commodity, it is limited in quantity, and we should treat it as such. He says we should spend the time we have wisely.

What does this look like in the Christian life?

* We will cherish the time we have with our children, mindful that they will quickly grow up;

- We will share the gospel message with our family and friends, knowing there is nothing more important than a relationship with Jesus Christ;
- We will make time to keep our relationship with our spouse vibrant and healthy because we know that a healthy marriage requires work and attention and this will enrich every other area of our lives;
- We will spend less time in fruitless pursuits (watching TV, browsing the internet, etc.) and more time doing things that matter (like spending time with family, seeking to feed our minds, or serving in a ministry that makes a lasting impact);
- We will work hard when we are at our jobs, knowing we are working for the Lord;
- We will make time for rest, recognizing God has not designed us to run non-stop;
- We will make corporate worship, personal Bible study, and prayer a priority for our time, because there is little else of greater value.

There are hundreds of different things that are competing for our time. Since time is like a valuable commodity, we must approach it much like we would our money. We must make a "time budget," recognizing how much time we have and prioritizing where best to spend it. Like in a financial budget, we pay our mortgage or rent, our light bill, our water bill, our insurance, etc. first. After that, we choose where to spend what we have left. We can do the same thing with our time. We should spend our time on the most important things first, and then looking at what is left, choose where best to spend it. Doing this may mean that we will have to say no to some good things because we just don't have time for them. We must choose the best things over good things.

Understand the Lord's Will

Paul's third instruction is in some ways a restatement of his first instruction. He says don't be foolish, but understand what the Lord's will is. A wise person recognizes that God's will must be best, and therefore we seek to do what God wants in our lives. We sometimes struggle with knowing what the Lord's will is for us in a given situation. Think about some of the questions that we typically ask:

- Should I take this job or not?
- What college should I attend?
- What should my major be?
- Should we move or should we stay where we are?
- Should I begin a relationship with this person or not?

Many people lament when faced with decisions like these because they aren't sure how to know what God's will is. Many books have been written about the proper techniques for "discovering" God's will for our lives. Knowing God's will isn't as difficult as some people make it out to be.

First and foremost, God's will is found in God's Word. Many Christians wrongly think that the only way we can know God's will is to pray for Him to reveal it to us in some spectacular way. We *should* ask God to give us wisdom and to show us His will, but we must do this while *also* searching the Bible for the answer! We have heard someone say God told them they should leave their marriage, or God said it was ok to live together with a person, or God told to me I should misrepresent my income so I would have more money to serve Him. I'm confident that God did not tell them any of these things. God doesn't contradict Himself, and He has already spoken clearly about many things in the Bible.

A wise person is able to understand God's will by looking at the principles given in Scripture and applying them in their life. If you are asking if it is God's will for you to enter into a relationship (romantic or business) with someone who is not a believer, you should know the Lord's will by knowing Scripture (Do not be unequally yoked). If you are asking if you should begin a romantic relationship with someone other than your spouse, the answer is clear in Scripture (Do not commit adultery.) If you are asking whether it is God's will for you to take a job that will require you to lie, cheat, or steal, the answer to that question is clearly given already!

There are some clear-cut answers we can find in Scripture regarding God's will, but what about the ones that aren't so clear-cut? What do we do when we are faced with a decision between two options that both seem good and on which Scripture is silent?

Notice the context of this passage. Paul's instruction to understand God's will doesn't stand alone. He has been giving us clear markers of God's will for our lives: to be pure instead of sexually immoral, to choose our language carefully and avoid being greedy. He has given us markers to show us His will—we can then use these markers to determine what the right path for our lives is.

In situations that aren't clear-cut we can make a decision based on what we know God wants from us and for us. We know: God wants us to put Him first, to avoid sinful behaviors, to serve Him in all we do, to care for our families, to be kind to others, etc. By looking at these markers, we can see the path God has marked off for us to travel. So when we face decisions between two seemingly good options, we must ask if both options will keep us on that path, or whether one will lead us off of it.

Let's take the example of choosing a college. Suppose you are down to two colleges, and are unsure which one to pick. You could ask several questions. Which one will help me grow in faith more? Will one draw me away from God? Does one have a vibrant campus ministry that will help me grow? Will one school challenge me to mature, both in faith and in life? These questions can help you discern if one or both of the options is leading you down God's path for your life.

Or suppose you are trying to decide whether to switch jobs. It is not just about compensation. See if the new job will help you move along the right path. Will one job enable you to spend more time with your family? Will one allow you to be at church on a regular basis? Will one be a better work environment—helping you to trust in Christ more? Will one job cause you to be pulled away from the Lord?

Sometimes asking these questions can help us make difficult decisions. They can help us to see whether one of the options leads us away from God. Sometimes both options seem to be on the path God has marked out. That's ok! We can ask God to guide us, and He might give us a clear indicator to guide us—and He might not. If He doesn't, I really think that either option is acceptable. Some people become paralyzed in these situations, worried that they'll choose wrong and mess up God's plan. Sometimes either option is good and God gives us the freedom to choose. We don't need to wear ourselves out worrying about it. That would be like becoming paralyzed with fear because you're not sure which socks are God's will for you to wear today. We see the absurdity when the decision is about socks, but the same is sometimes true about much bigger decisions. If we have honestly tried to seek God's will by searching Scripture and asking for His guidance, and both options still seem viable—they probably are! Our responsibility is to seek to stay on God's path and trust that He has a plan.

Paul's instruction to us is that we should be wise—understanding God's character, His desire for our lives, and His Word—and then live by applying that wisdom to our lives in the decisions we make each day.

Conclusion

The essence of Paul's instructions to us is to walk in wisdom, so it bears asking ourselves, how do we become wise? I think there are several things we can do.

First, **seek the Lord.** The ultimate source of wisdom is God Himself. There are two primary ways to seek God. One is prayer. James 1:5 says that if we lack wisdom we should ask God for it! God doesn't generally give wisdom overnight, but if we ask God to make us wise, He will do so. The second way is studying the Bible. I challenge you to make studying the Bible regularly a priority in your life. Don't concern yourself so much with the quantity of your Bible reading, but be more concerned with the quality of it. Read the Bible with the intention of trying to understand who God is and how He wants you to live. Seeking God may feel unnatural at first, but if we will continue to seek Him, we will become wise.

Second, **spend time with wise people.** We can learn a great deal from people who demonstrate wisdom in their own lives. Seek counsel from these people. Spend time with them, and learn everything you can from them. You will be surprised how much they rub off on you.

Third, **worship and study with other believers.** It is amazing how much more we can glean from Scripture when we study it together. This is why we place such an emphasis on Bible studies, youth groups, and Sunday School. These are places where we bring together people who desire to grow in their faith and walk wisely. You can learn a great deal about how to study the Bible by yourself by studying the Bible with other people. You may also be surprised at the wisdom you gain from the others in your group.

Fourth, **maintain perspective.** This is a difficult one. One of the challenges of walking in wisdom is we must guard against being driven only by our emotions. Remember, the choices we make have consequences; often consequences we may not always be able to anticipate.

Walking wisely is intended to protect us and guide us along the best path for our lives. If we remember this truth, it makes it easier to make the tough choices; those that fly in the face of conventional wisdom or prevailing opinion—and follow God.

Lastly, **make the effort.** Remember, wisdom is not just about having knowledge, but about applying that knowledge to your life. If you walk out of church today with a bunch of knowledge about wisdom but make no changes, you have missed the point! Living wisely is a lifelong process. None of us has "arrived". There is progress to be made in each of our lives. They key is to keep moving forward. Look at your life and find an area where you aren't living wisely. Focus on applying God's will in that area of your life. Over time, focus on another area, and another area. It won't be easy, and we will not do it perfectly. The key is to keep working at it. The effort we put in will eventually pay off.

The wisest decisions of all is to admit our sin and run to Christ for forgiveness. The Lord will make us into new people and give us His Spirit to live inside us. The Holy Spirit will guide us if we learn to listen. And if we learn to listen and follow we will discover the Lord's way of living is better than anything the world can offer.

Dig Deeper

1. What was the wisest decision you ever made? Did you struggle with it? How did you make the choice? What was the toughest decision you had to make and how did you make it? Looking back, do you think it was a wise decision?

2. Do you agree with the bulleted list of the kinds of decisions that are wise? How would you change the list?

3. How do you find wise people to follow? Who has been the most positively influential person in your life?

14
Filled with the Spirit
Ephesians 5:18-20

People long for joy. They want to find meaning, purpose, and enjoyment in life. Because of this, people look for joy in many places.

Some look for joy by amassing possessions, pursuing power, gaining education, or indulging pleasures. In the book of Ecclesiastes, Solomon says he tried all these things and concluded, "Everything is meaningless." When it was all said and done, he said, there is only one thing that satisfies: "To honor God and obey His commandments."

It is with that clear understanding Paul takes us to the next item in his list of things which are characteristic of the child of God. Again he points out the error to correct, the trait to pursue, and the results that will take place. Our text says

> *Don't be drunk with wine, because that will ruin your life. Instead, be filled with the Holy Spirit, (Ephesians 5:18, NLT)*

Avoid Drunkenness

Paul is not only addressing drunkenness. The tendency to look to alcohol to "take the edge off" is just one way people hinder the filling of the Spirit. You can be drunk with spending, sexual pleasures, work, power, activity, and even exercise (we will have to take your word on that one). Keep this in mind as we continue. You can substitute any of these things for "wine."

Paul does not say "Don't ever drink wine," he tells us not to do this in excess so that we become drunk. The abuse (or idolatry) of alcohol is not unique to our day. It has always been a problem. The Bible warns that leaders in the church must not be given to drunkenness. The reason for this, says Paul, is that it leads to debauchery or wild and unrestrained (or we could say "out of control") behavior.

Dr. Lloyd-Jones (who was a physician before he became a Pastor) writes,

> *Drink is not a stimulant, it is a depressant. It depresses first and foremost the highest centers in the brain. They are the very first to be influenced and affected by drink. They control everything that gives a man self-control, wisdom, understanding, discrimination, judgment, balance, the power to assess everything; in other words everything that makes a man behave at his very best and highest is what this part of the brain controls.[19]*

As a person drinks, they lose more and more of their "sense." If you have lived for any length of time you have seen someone in this state and know this is true. A person becomes verbally abusive, they do things they would not (and should not) do if they were sober. The person who is drunk may believe they are having a "good time" but the spectacle they make is quite embarrassing.

In times of drunkenness bad decisions are made. People get behind the wheel of a car in the belief they are unimpaired, engage in intimate behaviors (often with a stranger), and can say things that wound and can never be taken back or excused simply because "I had too much to drink." Because their reasoning ability is compromised, an inebriated person makes bad choices. Sometimes they have life-changing consequences! As our text says, "it will ruin your life."

This loss of inhibition is a wide open door for Satan to lead us into destructive behaviors. The loss of wisdom and self-control that results from overindulgence of alcohol undermines our walk with Christ.

Be Filled with the Spirit

Paul doesn't simply want to keep people from drinking too much. He gives us a better alternative: be filled or controlled by the Holy Spirit. Instead of being controlled by alcohol (or any other substitute), we should seek to be controlled or energized by the Holy Spirit. We should want to be "taken over" if you will, by the full power and presence of

God. The result of such filling is renewal, obedience, boldness, and a testimony that is powerful.

Every believer is given the Holy Spirit when they become a genuine follower of Christ. I believe this is what the Bible means by being baptized in, or by, the Spirit, or being "sealed" with the Spirit. These phrases describe our initial entry into the new life that comes through Christ.

Paul urges us to live under the control of the Holy Spirit as a regular course of our life. It is the antithesis to being controlled by a substance (such as alcohol or drugs). When someone is drunk we say they are "under the influence" of alcohol. Paul says we should instead by "under the influence" of the Spirit.

The word for "be filled" in the Greek denotes this is an ongoing process. We could translate it "keep on being filled." It is not a one-time experience but something we must seek every day.

J. Vernon McGee likens it to filling your car up with gas. When you head out on vacation you don't fill up your car and then forget about it. You have to stop and refill the car again and again. Or think of a glass of water. After you have refreshed yourself with a drink you will need to fill the glass again.

Every day (and often throughout the day) we must pray, "Lord, please open me up to receive the filling of your Spirit so that I might be controlled and led by your Spirit. We recognize we are most fully alive when we are most energized by Him. We are most effective as His disciples when we are most surrendered to His power and leading. This is what we should hunger for.

God is not reluctant, He is eager to fill us with His Spirit. However, for this to happen we must surrender to Him. We must give ourselves to the Spirit just like some give themselves to alcohol. To be filled with God's Spirit we have to "open the faucet" and allow the Spirit to flow into our lives.

Paul COMMANDS us to be filled with the Holy Spirit. It is something we have some control over. In other words, we don't have to wait for this to happen to us, it is something we can facilitate. How?

First, **we must stop grieving the Spirit**. We do this by not allowing lusts and passions to control us. In other words, we must pursue all these things that Paul has been teaching us in the verses leading up to this. We must pursue truth, control anger, seek forgiveness, and speak words that build up rather than destroy.

We had a faucet once that was shooting water in a strange direction. The water flow was weak. I checked out options for what might be wrong and finally took off the screen on the faucet and discovered it was filled with sediment. Once I cleaned out the sediment, the water flowed freely (I was pretty proud of myself for actually making a home repair). We must do the same thing in our spiritual lives.

When we choose not to listen to the Spirit, we "block the faucet." Hundreds of times (or more) a day we make a choice whether we will trust God or the culture around us. We decide whether we will copy the pattern of the people we admire (and from whom we want approval or acceptance) or copy the pattern of Christ. We choose between popular opinion and the Word of God. Every time we choose to turn from the ways of God we grieve or quench the Spirit. When we choose to follow His ways we allow the Spirit to fill us. We cannot be filled with the Spirit and engage in sinful or rebellious behavior at the same time. Sometimes people say, "God seems far away." Often that is because we have pushed Him far away.

Second, **we must be conscious of the Holy Spirit in our lives**. Think how differently you behave if you are aware your children are watching what you do. Or think about how you change your behavior if someone is staying in your home as a guest. When we have had visitors in our home I am very conscious of that fact. I try to be extra quiet when I get up in the morning, I am careful to set out items for breakfast and I plan my day based on the needs and desires of our guest. When we are aware of the presence of others we act differently.

We need to learn to be aware of the presence of the Spirit in our life! We take Him wherever we go! He hears everything we say...and think! It should be our desire to live in a way that honors the Holy Spirit living in us. This consciousness will help us as we make decisions.

Third, **resolve to respond to His promptings**. There are times when you just sense you should do something. There will be times when you feel a prompting to pray. When this happens, stop and pray. You feel you should read the Bible (it is astounding how many times you will be reading along and something "jumps out" that is just the right word for just the right time). You may feel led to call or visit someone, to give someone money, to ask someone a certain question, or you may be led to pursue a particular opportunity. At the time it may seem silly. Determine to be a person who is willing to follow where He leads.

Sometimes it may seem you were mistaken. However, the more you follow that leading, the better you will be at telling the difference between the leading of the Spirit and the wacky thoughts that sometimes pop into our minds. The better we are at recognizing His promptings, the more likely we will find His leading for the future. When we ignore the promptings we can become numb to them.

I can think of several occasions when I felt I should go and visit someone. One was a person I hadn't seen for a long time. I had heard he was in Hospice so I wanted to see him and unbeknownst to me, he was very near death. Another was a woman who was sick and when I arrived she was visiting with people. I went in to visit with her and said a prayer. In both instances I came in, spoke and prayed with the individual, and then they died! Everyone present was stunned at God's timing. But it wouldn't have happened if I didn't act on what I felt prompted to do.

When we respond to God's Spirit wonderful things happen.

- We know a supernatural peace when all around us are falling apart.
- We find the right words to say in a tense situation.
- We have a new clarity in our thoughts,
- We are tuned in to the heart of another unlike any other time.
- We have a boldness to stand for the truth of the gospel or to do what needs to be done.
- We know an uncommon intimacy with God and freedom in prayer.

The point is that we need to seek this filling. God will not often pour out His Spirit on an unwilling person. We must intentionally seek God's Spirit. Not only must we ask…we must be willing to respond.

Manifestations of the Spirit's Fullness

You can tell when someone has had too much to drink. Their face is flushed, their eyes may be reddened, and they may begin to slur words. They may be unsteady and start to wobble. They may have trouble paying attention, be uncoordinated, rude, giddy, or engage in inappropriate behavior. They may get sick and some will fall asleep.

When it comes to being filled with the Spirit, Paul says there are evidences of that filling. In Galatians 5:22 we are familiar with these words known as the fruit of the Spirit,

> *But the Holy Spirit produces this kind of fruit in our lives: love, joy, peace, patience, kindness, goodness, faithfulness, gentleness, and self-control. (Galatians 5:22-23, NLT)*

These traits should be seen in everyone who is a follower of Christ. When we pursue the fullness of the Spirit of God we experience these traits in greater measure. In our text Paul adds,

> *singing psalms and hymns and spiritual songs among yourselves, and making music to the Lord in your hearts. And give thanks for everything to God the Father in the name of our Lord Jesus Christ. (Ephesians 5:19-20, NLT)*

Most students of God's Word see three evidences of the filling of the Spirit in verses 19 and 20. First, **there is a love of corporate worship**. Paul says we will speak to one another with psalms, hymns and spiritual songs. This does not mean we will be quoting song lyrics to each other on the street corner (though that would be more edifying than most of our conversations). The picture here is that the Spirit will drive us together to worship the Lord.

Our times of worship are not obligations that are placed on us by the tradition of men. *Worship is part of the Spirit's plan for our growth and spiritual wellness.* Starting in the book of Exodus God laid out specific plans for weekly worship in the nation of Israel. It is part of God's vision for His people! Just as God gave us a day of rest, so He instituted the command for weekly worship. When we skip either of these things we resist the work of God's Spirit. This is part of the design and rhythm of life. When we pass on weekly worship, we turn away from the Lord.

Our *worship is valuable because we need each other.* God has designed us to be inter-dependent. He draws us together because in that togetherness we can learn from each other, pray for each other, and encourage each other in the path of discipleship. Corporate (or group) worship is something God established to help us in a practical way.

There is a growing group of believers who believe they don't need corporate worship. They are tired of church politics and bickering and believe they are being fed from the Internet and the media. Unfortunately, they fail to see their selfishness in robbing others of their influence and involvement. They are also missing out on the support, fellowship, and encouragement of the fellowship of God's people. What sounds spiritual is actually a seduction of Satan designed to undermine their growth and the growth of those around them!

The second evidence of the fullness of God's Spirit is a **new melody in our heart.** James Montgomery Boice wrote,

> *Paul is probably contrasting the edifying joyous worship of the Christian community, which has praise of God as its aim, with the destructive, noisy revelries of the pagan world, when people are drinking.*[20]

It is not music itself that is an evidence of God's Spirit; it is music which lifts our hearts in praise to the Lord. Music is powerful. Think about how a tune you hear in an elevator or on the radio can stick in your head for hours or days! Sometimes it is embarrassing what we absentmindedly are whistling or humming! (One day I was out mowing the lawn while absentmindedly whistling a beer jingle!) Music is powerful, it communicates on a deep level. Paul says those who are filled with the Spirit will have a new song in their heart.

I appreciate the fact Paul says Psalms, hymns, and spiritual songs. We can debate what each of these things mean but the bottom line is this: there are a variety of musical styles that can lift the heart to the Lord. It may be a Gregorian Chant, or a choir anthem of Mozart or Bach. It may be hymns from the hymnal that link generations, a brand new song from a contemporary Christian artist, or the sweet harmonies of Southern gospel. They are all tools of the Spirit when they direct our attention to the Lord. The style of music is not important; it is the way God uses music to draw us to Himself.

Third, the Holy Spirit will lead us to thanksgiving. The gratitude spoken of here is a gratitude that springs from an appreciation of the salvation that is ours because of God's grace. It is that overwhelming gratitude of one who has been pardoned minutes before their execution. It is the gratitude of the one who has survived a deadly fire or tornado.

As we experience the sweet and wonderful filling of God's Spirit, we become more acutely grateful for the position that is ours in Christ. This leads us to both humble and joyful gratitude. It is similar to that gratitude you feel when you first hold your newborn in your arms. There is a feeling of joy at the new life filled with the awareness of our deep unworthiness to be entrusted with such a precious gift. Such joyful gratitude changes the direction and outlook of our lives.

Conclusion

It is important we underline the point of these words with a couple of applications. **First, we are not left to follow Christ in our own strength.** At times, we can read the instruction we find in the Bible and feel completely overwhelmed. In our own strength we fall far short of the Lord's design for our lives.

The Good News is: God has not left us alone! He has provided us with the Holy Spirit to lead and empower us. Unfortunately, this is a resource left largely untapped. It is untapped because we are distracted by other things.

Like the rest of the world, we tend to turn to drink or other amusements to find happiness. You hear people say, "How are we going to have any fun if there isn't going to be any alcohol?" The irony is this: the way of the world produces deadness. It makes us progressively more unfeeling. The Spirit makes us more and more alive! I hope, like me, you are led to cry out more fully for God's Spirit to fill you and empower you.

Second, **the Christian walk is to be one of joy not drudgery.** Sadly, this will be a surprise to many. They think serving Christ is a burden to carry, or a sacrifice to make. There *are* sacrifices, but they do not lead to drudgery, they lead to the joy we are looking for.

Don't get me wrong, a life of joy is not the same thing as a life of ease. The Bible everywhere tells us there will be conflict. Trials are a part of life. They are used by God to make us grab more tightly to Him.

(It is NOT true that "God never gives us more than we can handle!" Often He gives us more than we can handle to drive us to Him! He wants us to discover His sufficiency.) In the times of greatest heartache we discover like Paul, "when we are weakest we discover His strength most profoundly."

Two roads stand before us: the way of indulgence and the way of the Spirit. We can be controlled by wine, riches, power, or any number of other indulgences, or we can pursue the increasing control and involvement of God's Spirit. One will lead to a hangover, the other will result in a depth of life the world craves, but will never understand.

Dig Deeper

1. What do you think most people are looking for when they drink?
2. What other indulgences might Paul use today as an example of something that hinders the filling of the Spirit?
3. What does it mean to "grieve the Spirit"? Do you think "quenching the Spirit" means the same thing?
4. What place does corporate worship play in being filled with the Spirit?
5. What counsel would you give someone who wanted to be "filled by the Spirit" in this way?

Bruce and Rick Goettsche

15
Treating Others in a Way that Honors Christ
Ephesians 5:21

When we try to describe what it means to be a genuine follower of Christ we generally turn to the truths we must believe. This is not a bad place to start. Paul spent the first three chapters talking about what a true believer understands and affirms. We must be able to distinguish truth from error or we will have no foundation on which to stand.

However, being a follower of Christ is not simply about data that must be assimilated. It's not about passing a theology exam. It is about actually walking with Jesus. A true believer is one who has truly trusted the Christ of the Bible and is learning to follow Him in the way they live their lives.

We must know the truth so we have a good foundation but that truth must also be applied in the way we live. The message that Jesus tried to teach His disciples and the religious leaders of the day is this: you are dealing with real PEOPLE! They are not case studies, problems to solve, or defendants awaiting a verdict from us on what should happen in their lives! They are people! They are wounded, broken, and often struggling.

When Jesus dealt with such people He did so with compassion, mercy, and grace. The people Jesus condemned were those who treated hurting people in a calloused way!

The true believer reveals him/her self as much by the way they live, as by what they teach. Both of these things are part of being a Christ-follower.

In the last half of Ephesians (where we have been) Paul is showing us what a true believer looks like in practice. He has given us a very specific list of the behaviors and characteristics of a Christ-follower. He is NOT telling us what we must do to be saved. He is teaching us what things a saved person should do. Though we all fall short of this standard, we should be making progress.

As we near the end of Ephesians 5 Paul turns to the most basic and important relationships of our lives: the relationships of husbands and wives, parents and children, and employers and employees. To begin the discussion he gives us an overarching principle. This principle (in verse 21) is the key to understanding the sometimes controversial concepts that follow.

> *And further, submit to one another out of reverence for Christ. (Ephesians 5:21, NLT)*
>
> *Out of respect for Christ, be courteously reverent to one another. (The Message)*

This simple sentence serves as a perfect bridge between verses 20 and 22. Paul has told us to be filled with the Spirit. One of the ways we evidence this filling is by this attitude of submission. It also serves as the principle on which all the following comments draw their life.

The Principle: Submit

The word used for submit is in a tense which indicates that submission is an ongoing activity. It is continuous. We are to "continue to submit to one another." Because the word is in the middle voice it indicates that it is a voluntary act; it is something we must choose to do.

Before we can submit to others we must first submit to Christ. We must be willing to follow His directions and trust His judgment. We turn to Him for salvation and we submit to Him as our Lord.

The best way to understand what submission means is to look at Jesus. Jesus modeled this behavior by giving His time freely to those around Him. He took the role of servant and washed the feet of His disciples in the upper room. He surrendered Himself to the will of God and embraced death on the cross in order to serve our need for a Savior. In Philippians 2 Paul wrote that by coming to earth to live as a man, the Son of God humbled Himself because He set aside the privileges of Godhood to take the form of a servant. Jesus gave us a pattern and an example of what it looks like to submit to one another.

In Romans 12:10 Paul says we should "in honor, prefer one another" and in Philippians 2:3 he says we should "(do) nothing from selfish ambition or from empty conceit, but in humble-mindedness count the other better than himself." Submission is about giving ourselves in service to the Lord and to one another.

This is a difficult concept for us because in our world it is power that is esteemed and submission is viewed as weakness. We are naturally selfish. In fact, it is encouraged. Society tells us that we should strive to possess servants, rather than to BE servants. We are constantly told to "fight for our rights" to "stand up for what we believe" and to "not let anyone push us around." We applaud such people and feel good when we feel we have stood our ground or won a victory against another (whether it is a clerk in a store or a corporation in a courtroom). The notion of submission is foreign to our thought process.

Paul is speaking to *every believer*. We are ALL to submit to each other out of reverence for Christ. This is where people get in trouble as we read the verses that follow. Paul is not simply telling wives to submit to their husbands, he is telling all of us to submit to each other!

This changes the way we read the verses that follow. We tend to read in terms of "what we are supposed to be getting, but are not." The attitude being encouraged is to look at what we can and should do for others. It is not about what I hope to get from marriage—it is about what I can give! That simple change in focus would revolutionize our marriages and families.

Keep this in Mind!

Before we talk further about submission, let's stop right here and dwell on the last words of the verse: "out of reverence for Christ." We are not told to submit to other people in response to their position. We are not even told to submit to those who are treating us right. When it comes to marriage we do not submit to one another because we are getting what we want out of the relationship. We don't submit to parents because they take good care of us. We don't submit to our employers because they give us good benefits. We submit because we love and worship the Lord.

How many times have you heard (or said), "I will submit to them when they earn my respect?" Or in marriage, "I will submit to them when they start doing their part in marriage?"

The reason we are to submit to others is because we love, trust, respect, and honor THE LORD! This is the way He wants us to treat each other. He calls us to be givers rather than takers.

If you bristle at the idea of submission, then you are fighting against the Lord! You are refusing to honor Him by serving one another. We are to serve each other...even when others are taking advantage of us.

What Does Submission Look Like?

Let's try to be practical and concrete. What does it mean to submit to one another? Let's look at it in terms of the negative and then the positive.

On the negative side, submission means:

- We will not push our own way on another.
- We will not be thoughtless. Most of the hurt we inflict on others comes from impulsive words and actions.
- We will not rank others. We will not determine a person's value based on their social class, job, income, IQ, race, gender or anything else. The submissive heart sees each person (including ourselves) as a sinner in need of grace, just like the Lord does.
- We will not be impatient with someone who disagrees with us because we are ALL in the process of growth. We can always learn from someone who sees things differently than we do. It is impossible to know which of us is farther ahead in our understanding.
- We will not pout (or punish others) when we don't get our own way.
- We will not assume the worst. How often have you misplaced your keys and your first thought was "who moved my keys?" We are quick to blame. Why do we assume someone moved our keys? Why do we think anyone cares at all about our keys? We assume a checkout person meant to overcharge us; that someone intended to get in our way; the person driving slow is doing so just to annoy us, and the waitress is deliberately slow in attending to us in a restaurant. The submissive person tries to give the benefit of the doubt.

The person who has the submissive mindset is like one who is a member of a military regiment. They understand that their job is to do what is necessary to win the battle. They view their fellow soldiers as brothers and they value and protect them. A good soldier understands that they are strongest when they work together.

The same is true in team sports. Any superior athlete has learned that they will only win games if the whole team is involved. Michael Jordan learned that he could not win championships by himself. He could set records but he couldn't win. As Jordan matured as a basketball player he worked to get everyone on the team involved early in the game. Team members must submit to one another so they can collectively gain victory.

With this in mind we can say that a person who submits to others is one who,

- Thinks about the needs of others before himself. They are aware that there are others in the room. They see where they can help and do so. They see beyond their own agenda.
- Recognizes that they can learn something from *everyone*. They remain learners. Even the expert doesn't know everything. It is easy to feel so informed that you view others condescendingly.
- Is willing to suffer if that is what it will take to honor the Lord.
- Walks humbly, aware that they are a sinner who has been saved by grace. There is no room at all for an attitude of superiority.
- Is willing to give up comfort, time, and possessions to help someone else.
- Focuses on the positive rather than the negative in others.

Let me be honest, I do not measure up well when applying these descriptions to evaluate my submission progress. However, my goal is not to present my experience, it is to present the Word of God! We all need a clear target to know what we are shooting at.

It is important that we add a caution here. Being submissive is not the same thing as being wimpy. Submitting to others does not mean we should compromise the truth in order to get along. We have no right to negotiate what God has told us is true anymore than a soldier has the right to change the order of a commanding officer on the battlefield! We may feel we are just trying to "get along" but we are really guilty of insubordination or even spiritual treason! God's truth is God's truth!

Remember, Paul spent the first three chapters of Ephesians underscoring the true way of salvation. We should alter our approach and even reign in our preferences as we submit to others...but we must never alter the truth of God! In the book of Galatians Paul said anyone who changes the truth should be accursed...or "go to Hell." The Bible tells us to contend for the truth (Jude 3). Contending for the truth is not the same as being contentious. Contending for the truth is not the same as contending for our tradition, our preference, or our political viewpoint; it means we must stand fast on what God has declared to be true.

Contrary to contemporary thinking, we are not being loving when we change the truth of God to be more "inclusive!" Only the truth will set people free. When we alter the truth of God, we actually withhold from others the way to true freedom. Our compromise may make them happy, but it will also keep them in bondage!

The Motivation Behind the Principle

Submission goes against our instinct. Athletes do what the coach says because they have learned to trust their coach. They understand that he/she sees the bigger picture. Submission is about trusting the heart and methods of our Lord.

There are two key principles to submission. First, let me state it again: **we will submit to others only to the degree that we have first learned to submit to Christ.** We need to learn to rest in, trust, and follow the Lord. If we have not learned to submit to Him, we will not be able to effectively submit to others in the name of Christ.

If we are honest, we will admit that we tend to "pick and choose" the commands of God we obey. We obey the commands with which we already agree. We obey commands that will get us what we want in our lives. However, when God tells us to do something outside of our "comfort zone," when He calls us to repent of some behavior of which we have become quite fond we resist, excuse, and rebel.

Learning to follow Christ is about trusting the Lord enough to do what He tells us to do. We trust even when we don't understand why He tells us to do something. It is about trusting His wisdom, His strength, and His love for us over our ability to understand. When we truly trust Him we will follow Him.

One of the reasons that Apple became such a booming company is because people learned to trust the vision of their founder, Steve Jobs. Some of his ideas, I'm sure, seemed crazy at first. However, the Apple team learned to embrace what Steve Jobs embraced. They discovered that he was able to envision what no one else could yet imagine.

Isn't it somewhat the same with the Lord? We need to learn to trust His wisdom over ours. God does not have the arrogance or personality quirks of Steve Jobs. He should be *easier* to trust!

The point is: until we learn how to submit to the highest authority in our lives we are going to have trouble submitting to anyone. Children who are not taught to respect and obey their parents will not respect and obey anyone else! We will really have trouble submitting to those we believe are inferior to us!

The second principle is this: **Submission encourages submission**. What I mean is this: as we learn to submit to the Lord we will be better able to submit to others. As we submit more to others, we will be better able to submit to the Lord.

There are at least two reasons for this: There is joy in submitting that encourages further submission. As we submit to others we will begin to see, understand, appreciate, and derive blessing from those to whom we submit. We will discover value in people we used to dismiss. We will test and prove God's faithfulness again and again.

As we submit, we discover the wisdom of God's direction and so we will follow it more fully. The more we submit to the Lord, the more we discover that God really does know what He is talking about. We will see His commands are not burdensome; they actually open doors and deepen our experience of life.

Where Do We Go from Here?

It is much easier to learn about submission in theory than it is to put it into practice. So let's try to be concrete. How do we begin to obey this command from the Lord?

First, start with your relationship with God. Submission is a spiritual trait. We will learn to better submit to God when we read the Bible not as a textbook but as a "playbook" for life. The idea of a playbook is to learn what you are supposed to do and what you are trying to accomplish. As you read the Bible each day, look for specific areas where God is calling you to live differently. Focus on one command that challenges you throughout the day and try to put it into practice.

Let me illustrate. Let's say you read the command "You shall have no other gods before me." Take time to think about the idols you may have in your life. What things have more influence in your life than the Lord? What things have the greatest control over your calendar, your money, or your emotions? It could be a hobby, a sport, popularity, profit, or even your children! These things quite likely are our idols and we must confess them and return the Lord to His rightful place.

Let's say you are convicted by His Word about speech or anger or any of the things we have been looking at in Ephesians. Remind yourself of these words often throughout the day. Be aware of when you discourage people rather than encourage them. Pay attention to when your words add to the flame of conflict rather than build a bridge to understanding and cooperation. Confess failures and seek God's strength to make corrections.

Second, look for ways to give your time and your energy to others. Submission is about recognizing other people as important. In other words, we learn to be submissive as we make time to listen. This doesn't mean we merely stop talking. It means to actually work at hearing and understanding what someone is saying. Work especially hard to listen to those whom you sometimes dismiss (they may be young, old, or have a very different personality from you).

Look for ways to help others in practical and simple ways. Hold a door, pick up something someone dropped on the floor, run an errand, empty the dishwasher, put in a load of laundry, clean up a mess, help someone out with a bill they can't pay. Often this is much easier to do with others than with your own family. In our own families we tend to tell ourselves "this isn't my job." We need to do what needs to be done (and try to do it cheerfully and without making others feeling guilty…which is harder than it sounds).

Deliberately ask others to instruct you. Ask people questions about their area of expertise. Instead of trying to show your competence, ask questions that will allow that person to teach you something you didn't know before. Instead of viewing this as a contest focused on "who knows more," deliberately take the role of a student. We all like to take turns at being "teacher." Being a student will expand us.

Share in another's joy or sorrow. When they rejoice, let them have the spotlight. Resist the desire to compare their joy with yours. Stop wrestling with them for center stage! Be gracious, let someone tell their story and share their victory. In times of sorrow work to understand the pain of another so that you can help carry that sorrow with them. Instead of telling them how to feel, let them tell you how they feel.

Do you know what one of the best ways is to give yourself to another person? PUT YOUR CELLPHONE DOWN! One of the most common complaints in marriage counseling is: "They are always on their cellphone!" This is also one of the biggest disconnects between parents and children: one or the other is always on their device!

When you put your cellphone down to talk to someone, you show them that they are important to you. When you refuse to play games while others are with you and when you let a call go to voicemail you show someone a conversation with them takes precedence over a conversation with someone else!

Monitor your progress in times of prayer. There is something wonderful about discussing things like submission with the Lord. When we inventory our own lives we tend to be easy on ourselves. However, as we evaluate our lives while in His presence, we see much more clearly. The Holy Spirit will open our eyes to the areas that still need work. He will also help us to see progress we are making.

As we make this a matter of prayer, God will mold our hearts. As He does, we will discover that submission is not a dirty word; it is a glorious secret that opens a door to a dimension of life few find. When this happens, submission will no longer be a duty; it will become a privilege and a joy. It will not only enrich our lives; it will enrich the life of everyone with whom we come into contract. And God will be pleased.

Dig Deeper

1. Has your view of submission changed? Did you see it as a positive or negative command in the past? What concepts were new to you?
2. Why do we fight submission?
3. Why is it harder to submit to someone you resent or resist? What is the real reason behind our reticence?
4. Do you agree that "submission" is the key to all our relationships?

16
A Good Command with a Bad Reputation
Ephesians 5:22-24

In this chapter we look at Paul's word to wives (men are in the next chapter). These words of Paul are among the most hated words in Scripture to many women. The reason for the hatred is twofold. First, sadly, this text has all too often been used by men to subject and diminish women. It has engendered some of the very attitudes that women have worked so hard to overcome. Second, the text has been woefully misunderstood and Paul has been shamefully slandered and dismissed.

If we read these words in context, we will see that God is encouraging both husbands and wives to give themselves in service and love to each other. Here's the text with a little more context. Paul writes,

> *21 And further, submit to one another out of reverence for Christ.*

> *22 For wives, this means submit to your husbands as to the Lord. 23 For a husband is the head of his wife as Christ is the head of the church. He is the Savior of his body, the church. 24 As the church submits to Christ, so you wives should submit to your husbands in everything.*

> *25 For husbands, this means love your wives, just as Christ loved the church. (Eph. 5:21-25, NLT)*

We cannot understand what Paul is saying to wives unless we understand the context of what Paul is saying overall. The overarching principle is in verse 21: we are to submit to one another out of reverence for Christ.

Paul illustrates the principle as it relates to wives, then husbands, then children, then parents, then how it relates in the workforce. In other words, this isn't about Paul "picking on" wives. He is applying this principle in all our most important relationships—the same mindset is being commanded for both the husband and the wife!

Paul is Not Picking on Women

Paul tells women to submit to their husbands as a way of submitting to the Lord. In truth, the word "submit" is not even in the verse! The word is implied from verse 21. So the text really says, "submit to one another out of reverence for Christ; Wives to your husbands as to the Lord (then later)...husbands, love your wives as Christ loved the church.

Women have worked hard for equality in our world. It is shameful that women were considered mere possessions by people. Even in the Bible we see women treated as less significant than men. However, what we see is the effect of sin rather than the creative intent of God. Men and women were designed to complement each other. God has been trying to move us back to that viewpoint.

Throughout the Old Testament when God dealt with women He treated them with honor. He heard the prayers of Sarah, Rachel, and Hannah. He honored Tamar, protected Rahab in Jericho (and placed her in the family line of Jesus). He called Deborah as one of the leaders of Israel in the book of Judges. He put both Ruth and Esther in the spotlight as women of faith. In a very male-dominated society God upheld the value of women.

When Jesus came on the scene He treated women as equals. He raised their status in the world. Mary and Elizabeth held prominent positions in the birth of Christ. Jesus talked to a woman in Samaria in John 4 that most people (even other women) avoided. He showed mercy to the woman caught in adultery. He praised the woman who anointed Him. Mary and Martha were prominent in his life. Women were at the cross and Jesus appeared first to a woman at His Resurrection. Priscilla was a woman who was prominent in the early church. Rather than subject women, the Church (and Paul) worked to revolutionize the role of women.

Many have called Paul a woman hater because of his words. However, Paul is the same man who wrote these words in Galatians 3:28

There is no longer Jew or Gentile, slave or free, male and female. For you are all one in Christ Jesus. (NLT)

The teaching of the church is we are all equal recipients of God's grace. That doesn't mean we are all the *same,* but we are all *equal.* So this command is not about "keeping women in their place."

What is Paul's Instruction to Wives?

Before we examine what the word "submit" means let's look at the "qualifiers." First, wives are to submit *to their husbands.* This is not about women submitting to all men. This is not a statement about a woman's value in the workplace or in society in general (I don't believe it is about a woman's value in the home either). This is a very narrow command.

Second, wives are told to do this as a way of showing honor to the Lord. In other words, this is a voluntary act of obedience. This is not about inherent worth, this is about religious devotion.

Again, we must remember that the word "submit" here is from verse 21. What we saw in verse 21 is summed up well by Tim Keller,

> *Paul is assuming if you're going to have a good marriage (verse 21), he's assuming you have a Spirit-created ability to be unselfish in the way in which you live. Stated negatively, this verse means the main problem in any marriage is self-centeredness. That's what kills marriage. That's what the heart of every marriage problem always is. That's the most basic problem you have.*[21]

A strange thing happens when we get married. During our time dating we celebrate all the great qualities in our partner and have a tendency to overlook or dismiss any negative traits. However, when we get married this often changes. We start to focus on the things our spouse is NOT doing. We complain about their weaknesses and flaws and completely overlook the very things that drew us to the person in the first place!

As a result we experience growing distance in our relationships. Respect is gone and honor diminishes.

Rather than being combative or negative in the home, Paul I believe, is saying, "Entrust yourself to your husbands, give yourself to them. Rather than straining for independence, trying to gain your rights and position...devote yourself to your mate. Instead of competing, work with and build up your spouse."

In Galatians Paul said,

> don't use your freedom to satisfy your sinful nature. Instead, use your freedom to serve one another in love. (Galatians 5:13, NLT)

Paul's entire argument here is for couples to approach marriage as a time of giving of oneself to each other with a selfless and servant mentality. (I happen to believe he is telling men the same thing in a different way.)

Different Roles in Marriage

People find Paul's words to be inflammatory when he says,

> For a husband is the head of his wife as Christ is the head of the church. He is the Savior of his body, the church. As the church submits to Christ, so you wives should submit to your husbands in everything. (Ephesians 5:23-24, NLT)

This phrase "the husband being the head of his wife" is a difficult one. Women react because what they hear Paul saying is: "Husbands are the boss of their wives and the home just as Christ is the boss of the church." I do not believe that is what Paul is saying even though I find the phrase a bit confusing.

It helps to understand that there are inherent differences between men and women. These differences are hardwired into us.

The brains of men and women are physically different.

Because of these differences men tend to get the gist of an issue very quickly but women tend to see the details. If you ask most husbands if they liked what you were wearing yesterday most of them would be in trouble because all we remember is that you were wearing clothes (we would have noticed if you hadn't been). Women generally notice the details.

Women tend to want to cooperate. They want to network and build teams. Woman naturally are better at negotiating. Men want to compete and win. If a man feels he is no longer in a position to win he will withdraw. He will take his ball and go home. (There is an interesting insight there ladies when it comes to motivating your husbands).

We are different by design. If we go back to Genesis we see that God designed men and women for different purposes. Adam was told to name the animals and work the ground. Eve was assigned to be Adam's helpmate. It seems God wanted husbands to take responsibility in the home and to lead. The wife was to encourage him in that area.

Before you react, ladies stop for a minute. What is one of the greatest problems in the home today? It is that dad is absent or disengaged. He goes to work, comes home, cuts the grass, perhaps grills out on the grill, and he feels he has done his part. Meanwhile, mom has gone to work, shopped on the way home, cooked dinner, bathed the kids, helped them with their homework, cleaned the house, managed the household calendar and then drops into bed exhausted. It has been my observation that most wives would like to have a husband who truly leads the family. But a husband can only lead if his family is willing to follow! Wives want someone who is engaged and involved. God wants husbands to be that way too. He encourages wives to help their husbands remain engaged. The best way to get men involved is to give them responsibility (and trust them to do it their way!) and to encourage them in the work that they are doing.

Let's make this more concrete. Men are competitive. Generally speaking, if they feel that they cannot be successful, they will disengage and throw themselves into some area where they do feel they can be successful. In other words, nagging and beating a man up because he is not doing things right will not encourage him, it will push him away! A man responds when he feels he is doing something right. You encourage Him by pointing out the good things he is doing! He responds when he believes his spouse views him as competent.

Let me give you a silly example. When my kids were born I made it a point to give them the first bath when they got home from the hospital. I wanted to help change the first diapers. This was not only because I love my children. I know me. If I waited to do these things, I would feel incompetent (compared to my wife), and would avoid doing it as a result.

Encourage your husband! Notice when he does things correctly. Ask him for help (rather than demand help). Be his cheerleader. Believe in Him (and then he will start to believe in himself). We need each other!

A Christian View of Marriage

There are still some people who rebel at this teaching. This is because we view marriage as a contest, or a battle for control.

The Bible presents a view of marriage that is different from the one popular in our society. Marriage for many today is "just a piece of paper." In the world's eyes we contract with another person and commit ourselves to a mutually satisfying relationship. When, or if, it stops becoming mutually satisfying, we divorce.

A contract marriage carries with it a list of expectations. Some of these are stated (I will mow the lawn, you cook the meals) but many others are implied (or assumed!). The result is that we live our married lives feeling that the other person is not "living up to their end" of the bargain. We *always* overinflate our contribution and we diminish the contribution of our spouse. The result is contention, frustration, and dissatisfaction.

The Biblical model for marriage is different. It is the idea of a covenant or promise. It starts with the idea of *mutual* submission. We do not look at marriage in terms of what we will GET (though most of us begin marriage this way), we learn to look at marriage in terms of what we can GIVE.

Here's the difference. In most wedding vows what people are really saying is this. "I take you to be my husband/wife in sickness and health, joy and sorrow, youth and old age...as long as it is still pleasant, satisfying and comfortable! If it is not, all deals are off!"

Marriage God's way is when we say, "I promise to be tender to you. I promise to be loving. I promise to be faithful. I promise to cherish you. And I promise to do all these things regardless of how I feel or what I perceive as your contribution to things. Christian marriage or covenantal love is defined in terms of commitment and a desire to meet the needs and encourage the growth of the other person.

Christian marriage is not easy. There are struggles in every marriage. Tim Keller helps us with a great illustration,

> *Here's a bridge, and there are all sorts of structural defects in the bridge, but you can't see them. They're hairline fractures. Nobody can really see them. A great big five-ton Mack truck comes over the bridge. When it gets on the bridge, it shows up all the structural defects because it strains the bridge and suddenly you can see where all the mistakes and the flaws are.*[22]

The truck doesn't create the flaws. It doesn't create the weakness. It reveals the weakness. When you get married, your spouse is this great big Mack truck coming right through your heart. Before you were married, other people tried to tell you about those defects. Your parents tried to tell you. Your roommates tried to tell you. You weren't in covenant with them. You could write it off. You weren't so intimate and so close that it really created problems for you: your selfishness, your fear, your pride, your bitterness, your worry.

You were never, even with your parents, in such an intimate relationship that those differences created problems for you. On top of that, if they told you about them too much, you could always leave. There was no covenant. There was no commitment. There was no vow. When you get married, it brings out the worst in you. When you get married, you will find in these close quarters the sins and structural flaws that were there but unnoticed.

The real mistake people make, almost always, is you feel like the conflict marriage has brought you into is a conflict with your spouse. Not a bit! The power of marriage is that marriage brings you into a confrontation not with your spouse; but with yourself. Marriage forces you to look in the mirror. Marriage gets you by the scruff of the neck, pushes your face in the mirror, and says, "Look at these things!"

Gary Thomas makes an important observation:

> *When I think my greatest need is to be loved and I'm not being loved by my spouse as I think I need to be, I become bitter and resentful. When I honestly believe*

157

*that I need to learn how to love, when I aspire to live
a life of love above all else, every day of marriage
provides ample opportunities for me to grow in that
need, which means I will appreciate my marriage
more and more. How much I accept this—my greatest
need—will determine in large part my overall
satisfaction in marriage. Show me a person who
thinks his greatest need is to be loved, and I'll show
you a person who often wonders if he married the
wrong person. Show me a person who truly aspires to
live a life of love, and I guarantee she is more
contented in her marriage than the average spouse.*[23]

Let me say a word to wives on behalf of your husband: We love you
and we need you! We need your help and we need your encouragement.
By nature, we will deny we need any help. We are geared to be
independent. However, underneath all the bravado, we know we need
help in developing intimacy. Paul is saying: Wives, stop fighting and
competing with your husband and instead encourage him and help him to
be a good husband and father in your home! Your husband wants this!
He wants you to be proud of him. He wants you to feel secure and safe in
your relationship. He wants to be a dad that his children can count on.
However, he often feels that he is failing and doesn't know what to do. In
those cases he will more than likely withdraw! The way to keep that from
happening is by letting him know that you love, appreciate, and respect
him. He needs to know that you are glad he is your husband.

And a word to husbands: keep reading! Do not walk away from here
with the idea that you are the King and your wife is your servant. That is
NOT what Paul is teaching! We need to hear the whole counsel of God!
Believe me...when you hear what God has to say to husbands, you will
realize that marriage is a partnership unlike anything the world knows or
can understand. You wife needs you to be a significant part of the family.
She needs you to love her and cherish her. She needs to know that you
are committed to her.

So let's work at this. God intended marriage to be the best of
relationships. For that to happen we have to stop competing with each

other and instead learn what it means to "submit to one another out of reverence for Christ."

Dig Deeper

1. Why do people react to the verse, "Wives submit to your husband?"
2. What is the real meaning of the idea of submission in marriage? How does verse 21 inform us?
3. What do you think the differences in the way men and women are designed mean for the roles God designed us to play?
4. Do you agree that husbands tend to disengage if they feel they are not needed or appreciated? What problems does that create? What are some ways to re-engage your spouse?
5. Do you believe men *want* to be great fathers and husbands but sometimes do not know what they should be doing? If this is true, what are some appropriate ways to encourage and inform husbands?

Bruce and Rick Goettsche

17
A Husband's Obligation to His Wife
Ephesians 5:25-30

We are in the process of working through a section of Ephesians where Paul is teaching us about God's design for relationships. These are important words and I have labored to show you that in order to fully understand them, they must be understood within the context of the larger passage. A failure to do so opens us up to distortion and in some cases, abuse.

The overarching principle is in Ephesians 5:21: "submit to one another out of reverence for Christ." In all our relationships we are to have an attitude of service toward each other. Paul is now applying this overarching principle to the specifics of marriage. He spoke first to the wives.

In the last chapter Paul said to wives: instead of trying to overthrow the leadership of your husband, encourage such leadership! Men are generally wired to push ahead and solve problems. If a man does not feel he is playing a significant role in the home, he will tend to disengage (and direct his energy to other things). Paul seems to be saying that encouragement will be much more effective than a competitive or critical spirit.

In this chapter we turn to Paul's instruction for husbands. Over the years some husbands have tried to use Paul's commands to control or make demands on their wives. We are going to see that these men stopped reading too soon. Much like the man in this story,

Jack Hayford tells about a married couple who had attended a seminar taught by a man who was determined to show that Scripture teaches that the man is IN CHARGE at home. It was the kind of terrible teaching on submission that turns women into lowly doormats. Well, this husband just loved it! He had never heard anything like it in his life, and he drank it all in. His wife, however, sat there fuming as she listened to hour after hour of this stuff.

When they left the meeting that night, the husband felt drunk with fresh power as he climbed into the car. While driving home, he said rather pompously, "Well, what did you think about that?" His wife didn't utter a word…so he continued, "I think it was *great!*"

When they arrived home, she got out and followed him silently into the house. Once inside, he slammed the door and said, "Wait right there…just stand right there." She stood, tight-lipped, and stared at him. "I've been thinking about what that fellow said tonight, and I want you to know that from now on *that's* the way it's gonna be around here. You got it? *That's* the way things are gonna run in this house!"

And having said that, he didn't see her for two weeks. After two weeks, *he could start to see her just a little bit out of one eye.*[24]

Of course women are offended by such teaching! If you listen to and actually hear the words of Paul to husbands—he puts everything into a much different light. He tells husbands how this command to "submit to one another" applies to them in their relationship with their wives.

> *For husbands, this means love your wives, just as Christ loved the church. He gave up his life for her to make her holy and clean, washed by the cleansing of God's word. He did this to present her to himself as a glorious church without a spot or wrinkle or any other blemish. Instead, she will be holy and without fault. In the same way, husbands ought to love their wives as they love their own bodies. For a man who loves his wife actually shows love for himself. No one hates his own body but feeds and cares for it, just as Christ cares for the church. And we are members of his body. (Ephesians 5:25-30, NLT)*

This was a radical command in Paul's day. In those days everyone believed a wife had responsibility to her husband (as a child to parent, and employee to employer). The order of authority was clear. What was startling about Paul's command was the reciprocal responsibility given. Paul views husbands and wives as equal partners in marriage.

A Husband is to Love His Wife Sacrificially

The first thing husbands are told is to love their wives. Too often men respond, "I love my wife, I married her didn't I?" Others point to the fact that they go to work every day and bring their paycheck home as evidence of love. But they are really missing the point. Paul qualifies his statement by saying husbands are to love "just as Christ loved the church. He gave up his life for her..."

Jesus gave His life to make it possible for us to be forgiven. He understood our need and addressed that need. Even now He continues to intercede for us. He has given us the Holy Spirit to guide us and to continuously pray for us. Jesus loves us with a sacrificial love.

Gary Thomas uses a word that may resonate with us more. He says we are called to "cherish" our wives. (His book should be required reading for every husband.)

The way we treat something acknowledges whether we cherish it or hold it with indifference or contempt. To truly cherish something is to go out of our way to show it off, protect it, and honor it. We want others to see and recognize and affirm the value that we see.

Just as an art collector will survey many frames and attempt many different lighting angles and then consider many different walls on which to showcase a particularly valuable piece of art, so when we cherish a person, we will put time, thought, and effort into honoring, showcasing, and protecting them.

...Learning to truly cherish each other turns marriage from an obligation into a delight. It lifts marriage above a commitment to a precious priority.[25]

Men cherish their cars, their time with friends, and even their workout times. But do we cherish our wives?

Here are some questions to ask yourself: Are you attentive to her? Are you eager to protect her from anything that would do her harm? Do you stand guard over her body and her soul? Do you take an interest in her? Can she count on you rallying to her defense whether the threat is from a physical attacker, a rude person or an insidious disease? Are you willing to give up what you want or desire (a new boat, a bigger TV, new golf clubs, or even a night out with the guys), so that you can show your wife how special she is? It may be using family funds to buy what she wants for the home, a weekend away, or even a night out with you. We show sacrificial love by...making sacrifices (and not making someone feel guilty for those sacrifices).

Tim Savage in his book *No Ordinary Marriage* gives some ideas I've adapted for what it means practically to love as Christ loved us.

- Jesus is never unfaithful. He is fiercely protective. He will do nothing to hurt us. In like manner a husband is to be faithful to his wife. We must stand guard over our marriage. We must guard the wandering eye. Savage writes, *"When flames of lust are ignited, when extramarital fantasies are entertained, when sexual purity is threatened, husbands must take quick, aggressive, and even ruthless action to distance themselves from temptation."* If we love our wives we will protect the exclusive nature of the relationship from anything that would threaten or diminish it. That doesn't just mean guarding against inappropriate relationships, but also inappropriate thoughts, fantasies, and behaviors as well.

- Jesus keeps us secure. He has promised to "never leave us or forsake us." He says nothing can take us from Him. Nothing will separate us from His love. A husband's job is to help his wife feel this kind of security. That means we do not threaten divorce or compare our wives to other "better" wives. We want our wives to know that no matter what happens we will ALWAYS be there for her; our commitment is not soft, but rock solid.

Jesus is attentive to the needs of His people. Just as Jesus noticed us, we need to pay attention to our wives. Men have a tendency to get so wrapped up in their own world of work, hobbies, and even sporting events, that sometimes our wives feel irrelevant. Men work diligently to develop things that are priorities to them. The problem is that sometimes our first love is our job, our golf swing, our

164

team's playoff hopes, or our favorite hobby. This needs to change! What would happen men if we pursued this deep, abiding, attentive kind of love with the same intensity that we pursue our work? You know what would happen...our marriages would be revitalized.[26]

A wife deserves to know that she is first (behind the Lord) in her husband's heart. Husbands, we communicate this by our behavior. Help out around the house. Be involved in the day to day issues of childcare. Pick up after the kids (or yourself). Be patient while she enjoys a day of shopping or a day pampering herself. Notice the things she does for the family.

Savage writes "A husband eager to plumb the innermost feelings of his wife, willing to turn off the television, rise from the Internet, return from work early, or delay a personal project in order to engage thoughtfully with his wife, will reap not only the satisfaction of deeper insight into the one he loves but also the reward of profound gratitude from the one whose life is now more fully known."[27]

Men, if you are paying attention you should already find yourself under some pretty heavy conviction.

A Husband is to Help His Wife Become All She Was Created to Be

When it comes to the church (or Christ-followers), the Lord is not content to merely sustain the life of those who have chosen to follow Him. He wants to "present her to himself as a glorious church without a spot or wrinkle or any other blemish. Instead, she will be holy and without fault." Jesus wants us to become what God created us to be. Husbands should encourage their wives to the same end.

Men, study your wife. Study them not only to appreciate them but also to discern their abilities and their strengths. As you recognize the gifts and abilities God has given your spouse, we should "fan the flame" and encourage our wives to grow in their area of ability or talent. How?

- Through our words. Tell them what you see. Affirm their strengths.
- Sacrifice to pay for further education if that is what is needed.
- Do the other things that need to be done to free them up to do what God gifted them to do (why can't a man clean the house, take care of the kids, do the laundry, drive to activities, cook meals?)
- Brag about them to others. Let others know that you are proud of your spouse.

Our wives should know that even if it seems like no one else believes in them...we will always believe in them. They need to know that we love to be seen with them. They need to feel appreciated, protected, and cherished.

Now, guys, let's be honest. Most of us are better at grunting than talking. We may talk about the weather or sports or our job. However, talking about feelings and showing genuine appreciation is something that is outside of our comfort zone. Part of the reason for this is that behind the macho exterior (for those of you who can pull that off) most men are insecure. Why? Because we know we are out of our league. We know we spend much of our married life without a clue as to what we are supposed to be doing. We feel inadequate in comparison to our wives.

So how do we change this? The simple answer is that we need to work at it. Just as we would work hard to develop any other skill, we must work hard at developing the skill of helping our wives feel secure, loved and encouraged. I am baffled sometimes at people who work hard at lots of things but treat their marriage as if it is something that should just "come naturally." So here are some suggestions,

- Read a book on marriage for your own benefit. I like to read marriage books to remind me of what I am supposed to be doing. (Try some of the books referenced in this chapter first.)
- Ask your wife how she prefers you put the dishes in the dishwasher rather than getting mad when you "don't do it

right." Your wife will appreciate the fact that you asked for direction.

- Intentionally work to honor your wife in public (and private).
- Rehearse positive things to say before you say them "live."
- Ask other people what strengths they see in your spouse. They may help you to see things you don't already see.
- Ask your wife what you do that makes her feel loved and secure. She may not believe you really want to know at first so don't give up! Likewise you can ask what you do that unintentionally may feed insecurity.

The early church father John Chrysostom urged husbands (speaking about their wives), "Never call her by her name alone, but with terms of endearment also, with honor, with much love. If you honor her, she won't require honor from others; she won't desire that praise that others give if she enjoys the praise that comes from you. Prefer her before all others, in every way, both for her beauty and for her sensitivity, and praise her."[28]

A Simple Principle

Paul appeals to men in a way they understand: "A man who loves his wife actually shows love for himself." Paul is not appealing to selfishness here. What he is saying is quite profound: There is great joy, contentment, and happiness that comes into our lives when we love, support, and encourage our wives. What we really want from a marriage is found only when we learn to give ourselves to our mate. Though it is true that if we adopt a giving attitude our wives will tend to be more responsive and loving, that is not the motive. The real joy comes from seeing someone you love become all God created them to be.

Think about your children. When you see them do well in school, or an athletic event, or even in business, aren't you proud of them? Don't you share in their joy? It is the same in our marriage. We should experience joy when we see our wives flourish because we love them. Will it mean they are a little less available to us? Maybe. But when we discover the joy of self-sacrificing love, we are willing to sacrifice our desires for the fulfillment of our wife.

In Conclusion

Paul wraps up his discussion on marriage with these words,

As the Scriptures say, "A man leaves his father and mother and is joined to his wife, and the two are united into one." This is a great mystery, but it is an illustration of the way Christ and the church are one. So again I say, each man must love his wife as he loves himself, and the wife must respect her husband. (Ephesians 5:31-33, NLT)

Paul brings us back once again to this idea of a covenant marriage. Marriage was never meant to be an arrangement...it was meant to be a commitment. It is in marriage that we learn what it means to love, to sacrifice, to communicate, to look beyond ourselves. It is in marriage where we learn about real discipleship. It takes work and determination to have a good marriage just as it does to grow in grace and truth. The song lyrics say "breaking up is hard to do." The only thing harder is staying together and really working at your marriage!

Isn't it interesting that in all the things he could say to men and women in marriage Paul boils down to two words: Love and Respect. Emerson Eggerichs has written a book on this and has concluded (as many of us discovered through the video series) that what men want/need most is respect and what women want/need most is love/security.

The reason we have so much trouble in marriage is because we spend so much time focusing on what we think we should be "getting." We feel disappointed, deprived, cheated, and ticked off. If we put as much effort into doing what WE were supposed to be doing as we put into grumbling about what we think our spouse is not doing...we would have a much better marriage and a much better life.

Both of us (Rick and Bruce) have seen our spouse turn away from us. We have seen what was supposed to last forever end. We have experienced the pain of rejection and the sense of failure. But we have also learned some things. Many of those things we have shared with you in these two chapters.

Let me say something to you who may be struggling in your marriage.

- Don't ignore what is going on. The idea that things are just going to go away is foolish. The reason some people say "I didn't see it coming" is because they were so deep in denial they did not see what was evident to others. Don't let your pride keep you from having a great marriage.

- Don't try to go it alone. We need God's help to truly love. May I be frank? If you are miserable in your relationship maybe the problem is not your spouse. Maybe the problem is that you are wrong in your relationship with God. Get your act together with Him. Listen to what He tells you in the Bible. It is almost impossible to forgive until you have known forgiveness (it is hard enough when you are aware of your own forgiveness). It is hard to love until you have known love. It is hard to see beyond yourself until you recognize that you serve at the pleasure of the King of Kings. A couple who is having trouble will inevitably drift not only from each other, but also from the Lord. They stop worshipping together, stop reading their Bible, and stop turning to God in prayer. Instead they spend more time with those who encourage them in bitterness and the sense of being wronged. I don't know what happens first (struggle in the home or struggle with the Lord) but for the relationship to be revitalized you need to work on BOTH areas.

- Talk with your spouse *calmly*. There is nothing gained by blaming and making charges. There is also nothing gained by pouting and the silent treatment. Beating someone up causes them to withdraw rather than open up. Lower the temperature of the conversation! The goal of conversation should be to understand (rather than "win"). You will get much farther in the conversation if you ask your spouse how YOU can be a better mate than in trying to FIX your spouse. Good conversation requires careful, very careful ...listening.

- Find an interpreter. This is a third party who is a believer and is good at really listening. In my experience many problems are caused by two people just not understanding each other. They misunderstand what is being said. Sometimes all you need is an interpreter. Most of my "counseling" is actually just helping people hear what is being said.

- Address serious problems seriously. If the problem is any kind of physical, sexual, or severe psychological abuse, you need to put some distance between you and the abuse. First, get safe. Then work to address the problem. If the problem is an addiction, you will need professional help and may need serious inpatient treatment. That treatment is not going to work unless the addict really wants to get well for themselves! God can change anyone! Even after very major problems, two people who want to save their marriage can do so by God's grace.

- Stop looking over the fence! It will always seem like someone else would be a better fit for you. That's smoke and mirrors! Lots of people look good when you are looking at them superficially. Even if the other person was as good as they look, you are bringing *your* baggage into the relationship. Any problem you have is not just your spouse…it is how you interact with your spouse. You will bring your bad habits into any new relationship. Work on the relationship you have instead of dreaming about a fantasy relationship you think you deserve.

Outside of our relationship with the Lord, marriage is the most significant relationship we will ever be involved in. The more we work at Biblical marriage the more we will grow in our knowledge of God. It is important for us to work hard at marriage. It is not meant to be a burden. Marriage was meant to be one of God's greatest gifts.

Dig Deeper

1. Husbands: What is the most insightful thing you learned from this chapter? Wives: What is the one thing from this chapter you would encourage men to underline, memorize, and put into practice?
2. How is it possible for someone to be committed to their mate and yet not cherish them?
3. Is there something in the chapter with which you disagree? If so, what is it? Why?
4. Go back over the action steps. Which one do you think will be the most difficult? Why?

18
Marriage and Discipleship
Ephesians 5:31-33

In the last chapters we have looked at the roles of wives and husbands in the marriage relationship. Paul's comments conclude with a brief statement in verse 32 that should cause us to stop and reflect on the depth of meaning in the verse. Let us read it in its narrow context,

> *31 As the Scriptures say, "A man leaves his father and mother and is joined to his wife, and the two are united into one." 32 This is a great mystery, but it is an illustration of the way Christ and the church are one. 33 So again I say, each man must love his wife as he loves himself, and the wife must respect her husband. (Ephesians 5:31-33, NLT)*

The question we pose in this chapter is lofty: How does marriage illustrate the union between Christ and the Church? And what can we learn from the relationship between Christ and the Church we can apply to marriage?

This is not a new idea. Paul has underscored this connection throughout his whole discussion. Marriage and our relationship to Christ are interrelated.

One Commentator writes,

> *The union of husband and wife, although sometimes imperfect, provides the best picture to describe the union of Christ with his church. "This is a great mystery" might better be translated, "There is a profound truth hidden here." As Paul contemplated the mutual love and loyalty...riches bestowed, intimacy and oneness, and self-sacrifice that should describe every marriage, he saw in these a picture of Christ and the church.[29]*

We learn several things from the marriage relationship.

We Learn About Grace and Repentance

You will learn very quickly in marriage that "keeping score" will destroy your relationship. When you do this, you find yourself always rehearsing past hurts and magnifying faults in an attempt to show that you are giving more than your fair share and getting much less than you deserve. In contrast, we are to treat each other in the same way that we have been treated by the Lord: with mercy and grace.

The only way for marriage to grow and flourish is to repent (truly acknowledge and name the hurt and express sorrow) when we have failed, and extend grace when our mate has repented. It is impossible to undo the past. No matter what pain we have inflicted or received (whether it was because of some relatively private sin or because of a horribly public sin), the pain cannot be undone. We have a choice: we can allow the pain of the past to destroy us or we can address the pain and move past it.

This is what we have learned about love from Christ. When we come to Him as broken people who acknowledge our sin and rebellion, we find grace and mercy because of the blood or sacrifice of Christ. We can't undo our sin even with all the offerings, good works, and meetings we attend. Our only hope is to turn to Christ for a grace we do not deserve and cannot earn. Repentance and grace are necessary ingredients to any truly loving relationship.

If you want to be part of God's family you have to stop trying to make things right (in essence trying to dig yourself out of trouble.) Instead, you must confess your sin, your inability to "fix things," and admit you need forgiveness and grace. When you come to Christ you find mercy and grace to help in your time of need.

If you want to have a strong marriage, you have to understand this and extend that same grace to your mate. We must forgive our spouse for those things done in the past. This means you have to stop throwing past failures in the face of your mate! Beating someone up with past failures makes it impossible to ever heal and move forward. We must treat each other the same way we have been treated by our Lord.

We Learn that Relationship Involves Sacrifice

When we think about two people becoming one, it is good for us to reflect on how we become one with Christ. Such oneness is impossible without the sacrifice of our Lord. He humbled Himself, became a servant, and then gave His life on our behalf.

In the book of 1 John we read,

> *God showed how much he loved us by sending his one and only Son into the world so that we might have eternal life through him. This is real love—not that we loved God, but that he loved us and sent his Son as a sacrifice to take away our sins. (1 John 4:9-10, NLT)*

The Bible reminds us that we are "bought with a price." Grace, mercy, and forgiveness are not without cost. Someone has to pay the price. The person who paid the price in our relationship with God is Jesus. Our forgiveness was costly to Him, and freely given to us.

We understand this idea of sacrifice in child rearing. We know (or quickly learn) that having kids will involve late night feedings, taking days off to care for sick children, sacrificing financially to provide what our children need, emotional sacrifices that come with trying to train our children, and adjusting our schedule to that of the needs of our children.

This same kind of sacrifice is needed in marriage. There is nothing easy about it. This is what Paul has been trying to teach us. Wives are to give themselves sacrificially for their husbands. Husbands are to give themselves sacrificially to their wives. Let's face it, we are happy to have our mates sacrifice for us—we are less enthused about sacrificing for them.

Where does this need for sacrifice reveal itself?

- When it comes to working through the pain of a deep hurt. Working through things like marital unfaithfulness, past abuse, and even hurtful words will require sacrifice. We must sacrifice the desire to get even. We must absorb the hurt (and that isn't easy).
- Financially (we may need to sacrifice some of what we want to support and encourage our mate).

- Emotionally. There will be times when we have to endure trying times (and sometimes hurtful words) in order to support our mate.
- In the use of our time. We will have to make quality time for our mate even though it may mean not being able to do other things (like the things we want to do). This especially means turning off our devices so we can talk to each other! You cannot truly communicate with another human being if you are distracted by something on a device! The other person sees your loyalties are divided and feels less important because of it.
- In family responsibilities. We should be willing to do what needs to be done in our household rather than insisting "That's not my job."

Sacrifice sounds like a "dirty word," but as we have mentioned before, sacrifice, submission, service, and the giving of ourselves is the secret to deep relationships and true joy.

We need a supernatural strength to make these kinds of sacrifices. Our relationship with Christ is an essential element to being able to do what needs to be done to build a great relationship.

We Learn the True Nature of Commitment

Marriage teaches us about commitment. As you enter into marriage, you quickly discover that things do not always run smoothly. There are days when we may not like each other because of some conflict or irritation. Increasingly, people throw up their hands and conclude they have made a mistake. They divorce and move on. That is not commitment!

The mistake is in our understanding of true love. When two people get married in the way God designed, they make a commitment to each other. Think about the words often included in marriage vows. ("for better or for worse, for richer or poorer, in sickness and in health, till death do us part.") Many people today seem to think the promise means: "I will do all these things as long as things are going well; as long as I feel fulfilled and satisfied; as long as the happy feeling remains." However, a true commitment is a covenant (rather than a contract). It is a promise that says: "I am committed to you no matter what happens. We will work through the times of pain. I won't give up. I won't walk away. I'm in."

That understanding helps us better understand God's love for us. Listen to these words from the book of Romans with the understanding we gain from marriage commitment,

> *Can anything ever separate us from Christ's love? Does it mean he no longer loves us if we have trouble or calamity, or are persecuted, or hungry, or destitute, or in danger, or threatened with death? (As the Scriptures say, "For your sake we are killed every day; we are being slaughtered like sheep.") No, despite all these things, overwhelming victory is ours through Christ, who loved us.*

> *And I am convinced that nothing can ever separate us from God's love. Neither death nor life, neither angels nor demons, neither our fears for today nor our worries about tomorrow—not even the powers of hell can separate us from God's love. No power in the sky above or in the earth below—indeed, nothing in all creation will ever be able to separate us from the love of God that is revealed in Christ Jesus our Lord. (Romans 8:35-39, NLT)*

God has promised to never, never, never leave us or forsake us! When we stumble...He is there. When we rebel...He continues to pursue us. When we become distracted...He continues to hold out open arms. God is committed to us.

This is the kind of commitment the Lord wants us to give to our marriage. This is also the kind of commitment He wants us to give to Him.

Being a committed follower of Jesus Christ is not about just showing up for worship when your schedule allows. (That would be like saying, "I'll be home whenever I can find time to be there.") It is not even about being present every Sunday for worship. True commitment is a day in and day out decision. Every decision will be impacted by our commitment to Christ. When we are truly committed to the Lord it will alter our priorities, our passions, and our actions – not just on Sunday, but every day.

We Learn that Love is Exclusive

From the book of Genesis, from the mouth of Jesus, and in the teaching of Paul we are reminded of this verse:

> *"A man leaves his father and mother and is joined to his wife, and the two are united into one." (Genesis 2:26; Matthew 19:5; Mark 10:7-8; 1 Corinthians 6:16, 7:10, 11; Ephesians 5:31)*

Jesus said "What God has joined together let no one split apart." All through the Bible God compared worshiping other gods to adultery. In the book of Hosea, God used unfaithfulness in marriage to illustrate unfaithfulness to God through idolatry. A love relationship will not tolerate rivals to that relationship. We cannot be committed to more than one person in a marriage relationship.

God calls us to be truly committed to Him. The Bible says "God is a jealous God." That is not a negative thing. It means God is passionate about guarding the special character of our relationship to Him.

When someone finds out their spouse was unfaithful, a common response is fury. The covenant of marriage has been violated. Trust has been trampled on. The feeling of betrayal and hurt is deep and devastating. Now get this: **This is how God feels when we wander off in our idolatry to serve other things!**

Let's turn this the other way. Imagine coming to Christ and saying, "Lord, I want you to save me. I want to be forgiven of my sin. I want you to give me a new heart. I want to know the joy that you alone can give. I want to hear your voice clearly in all that I do. However, I don't want anyone to know that I belong to you. I will worship you publicly only when it is convenient or I am in a crisis. I will read the Bible if I can't figure things out on my own. I am going to pursue all the things the world tells me will fulfill me and if they don't do the job I will turn to you. I want to fit in with those around me. I want to be like everyone else. I want your benefits but I am only willing to follow you on my terms."

How would you expect the Lord to respond to such a statement? He would say, "Come On! You can't have a real relationship without commitment. You can't 'sleep around' and still say you belong to, or truly love, me." *Marriage involves commitment. So does being a follower of Christ.*

Conclusion

We could continue to draw other lessons from marriage and God's relationship with us, but Paul's point is: we will never come closer to understanding the nature of a true relationship with God than through marriage. The Bible calls the church the bride of Christ. On occasion the Bible talks about God being our "husband." Marriage is the closest thing we have to the kind of love God has for us. *Rather than chafe at his commands to submit and to sacrifice, we need to see those commands as windows which will help us to experience and understand God and His love for us more fully.* Marriage is the laboratory for applying the principles of Christian growth and discipleship.

Let me conclude by speaking to two groups of people. **First, let me speak to the unmarried**. Some of you are unmarried by choice and others because of circumstances. It has perhaps been difficult for you to read these chapters on Ephesians 5:21-33.

Perhaps, you feel like a "second class" believer because you are not married. I hate to admit it, but the church sometimes unintentionally communicates this message. I ask for your forgiveness.

In 1 Corinthians 7 Paul says there are benefits to being single. Being single gives you the chance to serve God in an undivided manner. You don't have the same kind of demands that married people do. You can serve in ways most of us cannot. I hope you will learn about God from the example of marriage, even as you serve Him faithfully in your singleness.

The contemporary view of singleness is vastly different from the Bible's view. Society views singleness as freedom to do "whatever you want." It is about sexual license without the need for any commitment. This is a horrible perversion of God's design for our lives! Sex apart from marriage turns what was meant to be a path to intimacy into something that is a selfish pursuit of personal pleasure. Biblical singleness involves sexual purity. I commend those of you who choose to serve and honor God in your singleness.

A word to the divorced. I share an extended quote from Tim Keller because it is so compassionate and clear.

> *The Bible teaches, first, that divorce is an amputation. It's not like taking a shirt off; it's like taking an arm off. All this stuff we've been reading about the fact that two people become one flesh ... the head, the body, all this sort of thing ... proves why you have felt as maimed as you have. If we ever get to the place where our society and our laws try to treat divorce as if it's a light thing, as if it's a casual or routine thing, we will know they are lies because everybody who goes through it knows it's like an amputation.*
>
> *The Bible also teaches, just like doctors know, sometimes amputation is necessary to live. Nobody wants to take a leg off. Sometimes it's take the leg off or lose everything. That's the reason the Bible allows for divorce and regulates it,...in marriage you are so vulnerable that if a villain gets in there and starts to tear things up, you can be destroyed unless there's a divorce. That's why God allows for divorce on two grounds: adultery and willful desertion that cannot be remedied.*
>
> *Somebody says, "But what if I was the villain? What if looking back I'm the one who blew it?" Don't forget that Jesus Christ is married to you. The real marriage is intact if you belong to him. You're his bride, and he sees you through the rags and says, "I'm going to make you pure and spotless. I am devoted to you. I love you."[Even this sin is forgivable].[30]*

Our intention these last chapters has been to spotlight the beauty and majesty of what God designed marriage to be. Marriage is not old fashioned or outdated. It is not the construct of a Victorian and oppressive day. It is not something to be defined by lawmakers. Marriage is a wonderful gift from God that helps us understand more clearly what it means to be loved by God, what it means to love each other, and what it means to be a follower of Jesus.

May God help us to learn what it really means to be committed; to be able to see beyond ourselves. For, it is only when we see beyond ourselves that we can ever see the true majesty of Christ.

Dig Deeper

1. Why is forgiveness so difficult in marriage?
2. How would you describe commitment in marriage? What synonym would you choose for commitment?
3. Why does marriage require grace?
4. What does the exclusive nature of the marriage bed teach us about our relationship with God?

Bruce and Rick Goettsche

19
Instructions to Parents and Children
Ephesians 6:1-4

The parent/child relationship is one of the most unique and emotion-filled relationships you can experience. Children alternate between wanting to please their parents and wanting to get as far away from them as they can. Parents can look at their child with wonder at the gift that God has given them and can also be so frustrated with that same child that they would be willing to give them away to anyone who would take them! The parent/child relationship is filled with ups and downs, and it is deep and complex. In this chapter we look at some general principles for what we should be striving for in a good parent/child relationship.

Over the last several chapters we have examined Paul's command for Christians to submit to one another out of reverence for Christ (Ephesians 5:21). The last three chapters have focused on applying this principle to marriage. Now we turn our attention to the parent/child relationship. Paul gave instructions to both children and parents about what it means to submit to one another out of reverence for Christ.

Children

He speaks first to children:

> *Children, obey your parents because you belong to the Lord, for this is the right thing to do. "Honor your father and mother." This is the first commandment with a promise: If you honor your father and mother, "things will go well for you, and you will have a long life on the earth." (Ephesians 6:1-3, NLT)*

Paul says children should obey their parents because "it is the right thing to do." Even pagan cultures and systems of thought recognize that children need to obey their parents. Parents play a protective role, guiding and teaching children until they can take care of themselves.

Paul went back to the Ten Commandments and points out that God commanded children to "honor your father and mother." He reminds us that God said that if we would follow this command, "things will go well for you and you will have a long life on the earth." This is a general promise, not a universal one. When children die young or face hardship it isn't necessarily because they didn't honor their parents. What this promise is saying is, generally speaking, children who follow the instruction of their parents will face fewer hardships and less danger in the long run. The child who rebels against their parents by using drugs and alcohol, staying out late, being promiscuous, driving recklessly, and in general rebelling, is in much greater danger than the child who obeys.

There are lots of practical reasons to obey your parents: they have lived longer, have more experience, have made more mistakes, and have hopefully learned from those mistakes. They have greater wisdom than their child. But Paul says that children should not just obey their parents because it is beneficial to them. Notice what he says, "obey your parents because you belong to the Lord." The greatest motivation for children to obey is because it pleases God when they do.

So now we understand the rationale behind the command. Let's look at what this looks like in practice. The Ten Commandments say to honor your father and mother. Obedience is included within the idea of honor, but honoring your father and mother is more than just obedience.

You may have heard the story about a small child who got into the car and refused to sit in her seat. Her parents tried to convince her that she needed to sit, but she declared that she wanted to stand. Eventually the parents managed to get the little girl to sit down in her seat. One parent said to the little girl that they were glad she chose to sit down like they told her to. The little girl responded, "I may be sitting on the outside, but I'm standing on the inside!"

This is an example of obedience without honor. Paul says that children should not be grudgingly obedient, but that they should respect their parents enough to obey them, without complaining or arguing. Children should submit to their parents' authority, recognizing that God has placed them in that position to protect and guide them.

To this point, those of us who are parents have been nodding along, and some of you may have even wanted to shout out "Amen!" to Paul's instructions. But let me pose a question. At what age does a child no longer need to honor their father and mother? At what point in life does this command no longer apply to us? Even when we are parents (or grandparents), shouldn't we continue to honor our fathers and mothers?

The parent/child relationship necessarily changes over time, but the need to honor our fathers and mothers remains the same. It doesn't matter whether you are 5, 15, 25, or 55, Paul's instructions on submitting to our parents applies to us. As adults, we may no longer be expected to obey everything our parents tell us to do, but we must continue to show honor and respect toward them, and to carefully listen to the wisdom they share. We must recognize we honor the Lord when we honor them.

It's one thing to say we should honor our parents when they are good, caring, and selfless, but what about when parents are selfish, abusive, or have abandoned us? What do we do when our parents aren't Christians and oppose our faith?

I don't have clear answers for these situations. We are supposed to show honor to our parents, even if they are bad parents, but it will take a different form. I don't think you honor an abusive parent by allowing them to continue abusing you. It's important for a child whose parent is abusing them to get help and to find safety. Some may not even have a relationship with parents because they walked out or treated you shamefully. Paul is not saying that we must be doormats.

Paul is saying we should try to find ways to honor the parents God has given us. For some, that may mean starting by praying for them. Pray God would help them to understand His love as you have. Pray God's love will win and change their heart. Pray that somehow He would heal your relationship. Sometimes we start by simply being civil. Rather than attack your parents, choose to be polite.

If you are in a situation like this, it saddens me. It isn't the way this relationship should be. I encourage you to seek the Lord's will on how you can show some kind of honor to your parents—even if it falls far short of what you would like that relationship to be. The key is to *do what we can* to honor them. Ultimately, we do not honor our parents because they deserve it, but because when we do so, we honor the Lord.

Parents

Paul doesn't stop with just instructing children about how to submit to their parents. He turns the tables and tells parents that, in a sense, they should submit to their children.

> *Fathers, do not provoke your children to anger by the*
> *way you treat them. Rather, bring them up with the*
> *discipline and instruction that comes from the Lord.*
> *(Ephesians 6:4, NLT)*

This command is addressed to fathers, but it applies to both mothers and fathers. Paul says parents should be careful in the way they treat their children. They should train their children in the right way to live, and do so in a way that shows respect for the child, and avoids wounding their spirit.

In Paul's day, this was a radical departure from societal norms. In Roman society, the father had absolute authority over his children throughout their lives. A father could command his children to do whatever he wanted, and they were expected to comply, no matter what. A father could do whatever he wanted to his children (including killing them) because they belonged to him alone. Children were seen as the property of their fathers.

In Paul's day, the notion that parents should be considerate of their children's feelings would have been radical. Today, that notion is not so radical—the pendulum has almost swung to the opposite extreme. Today's society encourages parents to be their children's best friend. This means (I am gathering) we should not anger our children and let them experiment and find their own way. That isn't what Paul is saying either. Paul's instructions to parents falls somewhere between these two extremes.

Paul says that parents should train their children but not provoke them to anger. Every parent knows that sometimes it is necessary to do something that will make your child angry. Paul isn't saying we should avoid making our children angry at all costs. He is saying we should train our children in a way that respects them as people. That means we must pay attention to our tone as we relate to our children. We should train our children without belittling or humiliating them. We should avoid teasing, sarcasm, and abuse. Dr. James Dobson said it well: we should mold our child's will without breaking their spirit.

The negative command is to not provoke our children to anger, but Paul also gives a positive command. He says parents should "bring [their children] up with the discipline and instruction that comes from the Lord." That means we have two primary responsibilities. The first is that **we should bring our children up in the way of the Lord.** The phrase, "bring them up" carries the idea of nourishing or feeding our children. As parents, we must take the time to nourish our children, not just physically and mentally, but also spiritually. We must teach them about what it means to be a Christian and help to instill biblical truth into their lives. It is not enough to simply drop your kids off at church, Sunday School, AWANA, and Youth Group. Those things are great ways to help nourish your children, but they can't grow on just one or two meals a week! The programs at the church should build on the foundation you are laying at home.

We have the opportunity to bring up our children in the way of the Lord by the way we live every day. Listen to what God told the Israelites to do in this regard.

> *Listen, O Israel! The LORD is our God, the LORD alone. And you must love the LORD your God with all your heart, all your soul, and all your strength. And you must commit yourselves wholeheartedly to these commands that I am giving you today. Repeat them again and again to your children. Talk about them when you are at home and when you are on the road, when you are going to bed and when you are getting up. (Deuteronomy 6:4-7, NLT)*

God gave the Israelites commands, told them to be committed to those commands, and then to continually share them with their children. We should do the same today. We must seize opportunities to share Scriptural truths with our children. We don't have to preach sermons to our kids (they aren't effective anyway), but we can help them learn to think biblically in the course of everyday life. Here are some ideas to get you started.

- Pray with your children regularly. Pray before meals, before they go to bed, before a big test or a big decision. Help them learn to turn to the Lord first.
- Read the Bible to or with your children regularly. Make it a regular part of your bedtime routine. Do a family devotion around the dinner table. Find ways to teach your children the importance of studying the Bible regularly.
- Bring biblical principles to bear on the situations you discuss around the dinner table. When your child talks about another child being bullied, remind them that God loves us and wants us to show love to others. When they talk about cheating, remind them God wants us to be honest. When they mess up, remind them God offers us forgiveness for our sins, and we forgive them too. Help them see the impact of the gospel message.
- Teach financial stewardship by encouraging your children to give a portion of their allowance or paycheck to the Lord. Show them how you decide how much to give and encourage them to follow the same pattern.
- Interact with the television shows or movies you watch. Point out the non-Christian (or anti-Christian) values that are being espoused. Explain what God says about these things, and why He says them. Help your children see there is another perspective besides what is shown on TV.
- As you work together on a project around the house or even a school assignment, remind your child that God wants us to do our best all the time, because we should always work as though we are doing it for Him.

These are only a few examples. There are many more. The goal is to create an environment where discussions about Christianity are commonplace. Our homes should be places where our children feel safe to ask questions about faith, and where they see faith impacting every aspect of our lives.

It seems obvious, but it needs to be said: If we are going to lead our children in the way of the Lord, we must be walking in that way ourselves! Our children will learn as much from our examples as they will from our words. When they see us trying to live a godly life, it will help them see that being a Christian is not just about going to church on Sunday, it is about the way we live in every area of life! Likewise if they hear us talk but don't see it practiced, this will turn them away from the Lord.

Francis and Lisa Chan wrote,

> *They will eventually get to the age where they can reason logically and ask themselves why we spent so much time playing as a family when we knew that so many on earth were suffering, dying, and headed for hell. Maybe this is why 75 percent of church-raised children ditch the church when they turn 18. They see the gap between our supposed beliefs and our actions and decide not to join the hypocrisy.[31]*

Simple truths lived out and repeated over and over will have a greater impact on teaching our children to live according to God's commands than almost anything else we can do.

The second responsibility is to discipline and instruct. We are to train our children in the right ways to live. Often discipline is unpleasant at the time, but we understand that it is a necessary part of training our children. Sometimes we must punish children for misbehaving. But we should also praise our children when they do the right things. We need to help them see the progress they've made in some areas while also helping them to focus on the areas that still need work.

How do we do this? We must see the big picture. As we train our children, we need to keep in mind what we want them to learn. Our discipline needs to be intentional. When we tell our children to do something, we need to be prepared to explain why it is important for them to obey us. We must seek to avoid telling our children to do something simply, "Because I said so!" While at some point, children do need to simply obey their parents even if they don't understand, we must remember that one of the ways we can train our children is to explain to them why we are telling them to do something. It can be as simple as, "Don't jump on the couch because you might hurt yourself or someone else." or "You need to be home by your curfew because we have plans early in the morning." Even when we explain our reasons, children will not always understand or appreciate them at the time, and sometimes we must compel them to obey, but ultimately we must discipline our children with a purpose—to instill Godly principles of how to live into their lives.

Again, let me quote the Chans,

> *I have never allowed any of my children to speak disrespectfully to Lisa or myself. We exercise authority so they have a picture of authority. It's not about a power trip. As a dad, my job is to paint a picture of God by the way I act. Since we do not worship a weak God who permits disrespect, I refuse to be a weak dad who allows his kids to talk back. Children who grow up ruling the house will soon find themselves questioning God's right to give commands that go against how they think or feel. Those who grow up in a home where loving leadership is exemplified are not guaranteed to respect God, but at least they know how it would look.[32]*

Sometimes it is necessary to punish children in order to train them. Punishing misbehavior is an area where we can provoke our children to anger if we aren't careful. I've condensed some wisdom from Dr. D. Martyn Lloyd-Jones on what we should strive for when we must punish our children.

We should be controlled. We should not punish our children in a rage, because then our concern is not to train our children, but to vent our anger. Before we can control our children's behavior, we must control our own behavior. We must compose ourselves and think clearly before we impose any punishment on our children.

We should be consistent. Our expectations for our children cannot change from day to day. If a child is punished for doing something on one day and then is told that the same behavior is acceptable the next, they will quickly become frustrated! We must be consistent by doing the same things we expect our children to do. If we are trying to teach our children to behave in the right way, they should see us living that way too. When we tell our children they must do something but then we do the opposite, it sends the message that it's not really important. One example of this we often see is in regards to church attendance. Kids ask, "Why do I have to go to church if Dad (or Mom) doesn't?" We must model the kind of behavior that we expect from our children.

We should be considerate. We must consider each situation and each child carefully. This means that the punishment should fit the crime, and it should also fit the child. We should take time to hear our child's side of the story and then impose discipline in the way that we think is most appropriate. We will punish differently when a child is trying to do what is right but chose poorly than when the child is acting in open defiance. We must consider all angles of the situation before we blindly impose disciplinary measures.

There is yet another side to discipline. It is not simply about correcting bad behavior or setting down good rules for them to follow. We also teach our children to be disciplined in: following through on jobs, reading the Bible regularly, eating well, getting exercise, being a good steward of all God has given us, and making good choices (sometimes we need to turn off the TV or gaming system).

When we don't take the time to teach these things to our children, someone else will swoop in and pollute their minds. We must be proactive in training. It is up to us to answer or find answers to the questions asked by our children.

Conclusion

As we saw in the passages on marriage, the principle of mutual submission impacts every area of our lives. Children must submit to their parents because doing so honors God, and it will be beneficial for them. Parents must submit their own desires and comfort to their children's need for instruction and nourishment, gently molding them into the person God wants them to be.

A great question Francis Chan asked in his book: "What will break my heart more? If my kids end up not loving me? Or if they end up not loving the Lord? The question points to the eternal significance of what we are doing as parents. Eternity hangs in the balance! We cannot afford to live only for the moment or lose sight of the goal. Parenting is a huge responsibility.

These commands are not easy to apply. They require us to see beyond ourselves and sacrifice our own desires for the benefit of others. Ultimately, we see the example of how to do this in God himself. He loved us and showed it by sacrificing His life for us. In whatever role we occupy in life, whether parent or child, husband or wife, or anywhere else, we must strive to follow the example God has given us; to love others enough that we sacrifice our own desires and comforts for their greater benefit.

Dig Deeper

1. What advice would you give a teenager about relating to their parents from this chapter?
2. What would you say to the parent who is overly strict and controlling? The parent who seems to have no rules at all?
3. In what ways have you tried to lead your family in the way of discipleship? How have you fared?
4. In what ways do parents lead their children *away* from Christ without even realizing it?
5. What is the most important lesson you want to remember from this passage?

20
Working for the Glory of God
Ephesians 6:5-9

We have belabored the point that true Christian faith leads to a change in values, orientation and behavior. This change in orientation is not the *cause* of our salvation; but the *result* of it. It is something brought about by the Holy Spirit living inside of us.

The Holy Spirit changes us in our relationships. The overarching principle is found in Ephesians 5:21: "Submit yourselves to each other out of reverence for Christ." Christian people are to be givers rather than takers. We view and treat others as wonderfully valuable.

Paul has applied this principle to husbands and wives and then to parents and children, and in this chapter we look at the change in relationships in the workplace. First, let's read the text.

> *⁵ Slaves, obey your earthly masters with deep respect and fear. Serve them sincerely as you would serve Christ. ⁶ Try to please them all the time, not just when they are watching you. As slaves of Christ, do the will of God with all your heart. ⁷ Work with enthusiasm, as though you were working for the Lord rather than for people. ⁸ Remember that the Lord will reward each one of us for the good we do, whether we are slaves or free.*
>
> *⁹ Masters, treat your slaves in the same way. Don't threaten them; remember, you both have the same Master in heaven, and he has no favorites. (Ephesians 6:5-9, NLT)*

Anytime this text is read the same question is raised:

Why Didn't Paul Out Speak Against Slavery?

There have been some (Pastors included) who have viewed this text as a justification for slavery (mostly in the time before and during the Civil War). Others have viewed this as justification for class distinctions. There are some people today who dismiss the Bible as truly God's Word because Paul (and others) did not "condemn slavery."

Slavery was Different. In the world in which Paul was living as many as 1/3 of the people in the Roman Empire were slaves (some have estimated 60 million people). Commentators say that when Paul wrote this letter slavery was radically different from what it was in America. Kent Hughes writes,

> Slaves under Roman law in the first century could generally count on eventually being set free. Very few ever reached old age as slaves. Slave owners were releasing slaves at such a rate that Augustus Caesar introduced legal restrictions to curb the trend. Despite this, inscriptions indicate that almost 50 percent of slaves were freed before the age of thirty. What is more, while the slave remained his master's possession he could own property — including other slaves! — and completely controlled his own property, so that he could invest and save to purchase his own freedom.

> We also must understand that being a slave did not indicate one's social class. Slaves regularly were accorded the social status of their owners. Regarding outward appearance, it was usually impossible to distinguish a slave from free persons. A slave could be a custodian, a salesman, or a CEO. Many slaves lived separately from their owners. Finally, selling oneself into slavery was commonly used as a means of obtaining Roman citizenship and gaining an entrance into society. Roman slavery in the first century was far more humane and civilized than the American/African slavery practiced in this country much later. This is a sobering and humbling fact![33]

The slavery in Paul's day was much closer to our employer/employee relationships than it was to the slavery that we generally think of. However, there were abuses. People were victimized. So, why didn't Paul address these facts?

A second consideration is that **change takes time**. Much of the economic stability of people (including the slaves themselves) was tied to slavery. If slavery were immediately eliminated, people would be out of work, could not care for their families, and production would be deeply hampered. (Imagine if the law said, "You can no longer have employees because it was thought to diminish people, you can only have business partners." The result would be that many businesses would close and way too many people would lose their jobs.)

Paul understood that the first step to real change in society is a change in the heart. Paul understood that Christianity, rightly applied, would lead to greater equality and dignity among people. When the human heart changes, a person's values will also change. When values change, people behave and relate to others differently.

Maybe there is a message to us. We cannot legislate a change of heart and values. We are better served to give more energy to pointing people to a genuine encounter with Jesus than in railing against the issues of the day. We should continue to push for change, but with the understanding that desiring a change in values without a change of heart is futile. Paul was more concerned about winning the war than winning this one battle. That should be our goal also.

How Does the Principle of Mutual Submission Apply on The Job?

There are two WRONG views of work:

1. Work is a curse and leisure is the meaning of life. In other words, we work so we will get paid and then be able to enjoy life. Work is a necessary evil.
2. Work is the meaning of life. In other words work is everything. The job, status, titles, income of a person is their measure of worth. The person with the most power is the one who has the

most significance. (These people are often the ones who are "working themselves into the ground.")

The Bible views work as a joy; it's a way to contribute to the world and demonstrate honor to the Lord. The Christian desires to honor the Lord in whatever job he/she is doing.

Paul gives at least four guidelines to those who work for someone else. The first is: **Do your job.** We are to obey those in authority over us. If we translate this to work it would mean: we should do our job. If you agree to do a particular job then you should do what you agreed to do.

This seems obvious, but we all know that there are some who have the attitude that they should do the least they can possibly do and still get paid. You see people doing any number of things other than their job while they are "on the clock." This is dishonest and it is taking advantage of the one who is paying us a salary.

Second, **we are to show respect and honor to those in authority over us.** The Bible tells slaves to serve in "reverent fear." This is not "fear" in the sense of terror; it is respect. Think about the fear you have for a police officer sitting on the side of the road as you are driving by. Your fear comes from a respect which recognizes the authority the officer has to enforce the law (and a realization that you may be breaking that law).

We are to respect the fact that our employer has authority to terminate our employment. We respect the fact that the person owns the business carries the responsibility for how the business is run. Practically, this means that we speak to our employer with respect and we should speak *about* our employer to others with respect. If you are running down your employer, you are not a very good employee since you are representing the business in a bad light.

Third, **work for the Lord, not your employer.** I don't mean that you should spend all your time witnessing and sharing the Bible with others. It means that the way we work will either honor or dishonor the Lord. We need to understand that the way we work reveals a great deal about the nature of faith.

Ask yourself some questions: Is God honored by the way I do my job? Can people see the influence of Christ in my life by the way that I work, by the things that I say, and by the way that I treat those around me? Am I giving God my best or am I giving Him only enough to "get by"?

> *William Carey was a shoemaker who applied to go out as a foreign missionary. Someone asked him, "What is your business?" meaning to humiliate him, because he was not an ordained minister. Carey answered, "My business is serving the Lord, and I make shoes to pay expenses."[34]*

Carey had the right attitude.

The Westminster Shorter Catechism states as its first question: "What is the chief end of man? It is to glorify God and to enjoy Him forever." Our job is to glorify God in everything we do. Our place of employment is the platform by which we do this.

The fourth principle is: **Be Consistent**. Paul tells us to "please them all the time, not just when they are watching you." Let's go back to the police officer with the radar gun along the side of the road. A true law-abiding driver is one who obeys the law ALL THE TIME not just when they see a police officer!

Think about a class of students. Let's say you have a PE class. You tell the kids that they need to run around the gym. They grumble and start running. You have to step out for a couple of minutes. What is going to happen in the class? Many of the students, perhaps even most of the students will stop running and start walking slowly. Some might even stop to visit. They will only run again when the teacher comes back into the gym. Paul says we should be workers who do a good job whether anyone is watching or not.

Who we are when no one else is looking is, quite frankly, who we really are. We can try to sell a certain image of ourselves to others. But that is not who we really are. Character and integrity will eventually show themselves for what they are. Paul says, "In whatever you do, do it all for the glory of God." (Colossians 3:23, paraphrase) You may be able to fool your earthly employer, but you don't fool the Lord.

How Does the Principle of Submission Apply to Those in Charge?

Paul doesn't speak only to the workers; he also speaks to those who are in authority over the workers. In each of these examples (husband and wife, parent and child, and now boss and worker) Paul shows that the servant attitude is important on both sides of the relationship.

To those who have authority over people Paul has some counsel. He begins with the words, "in the same way." We might say, "In the same way as what?" I believe Paul is saying that **this principle of submission and giving of yourself applies in the same way to those who have authority over others**. Practically, this means

- Treat those under you with the same respect and dignity that you desire in return.
- Treat those under you as people of value rather than as things you own.
- Realize that the people under you are given to you by God to care for and encourage their growth in the Lord and as people.

Paul says, "Don't threaten them; remember you both have the same Master in heaven, and he has no favorites." I see two more principles here: **Show respect for workers and treat them with dignity.**

Dennis Bakke who founded a company called AES (Alternative Energy Source) built the company on a different model than most businesses. He writes,

> A special workplace has many ingredients. The feeling that you are part of a team, a sense of community, the knowledge that what you do has real purpose—all these things help make work fun. But by far the most important factor is whether people are able to use their individual talents and skills to do something useful, significant, and worthwhile. When bosses make all the decisions, we are apt to feel frustrated and powerless, like overgrown children being told what to do by our parents. [35]

These are good insights. They remind us that treating people with dignity means helping them take pride and ownership in the work that they do. It means putting people in positions where they can succeed and contribute to the work in a significant way. We do this by encouraging people to be part of the process rather than merely imposing rules on them.

Treating people with dignity means we live with the conviction people are more important than profit. It is paying a fair wage, training people adequately, being supportive in times of personal crisis, and viewing these people as part of the team rather than as property you own. Obviously, a business needs to make money in order to stay in business. However, the question is: is our drive for profit coming at the expense of the dignity and value of the people who work for us?

Paul says we need to **remember that we both have the same Master in heaven**. Paul reminded employers that God does not play favorites. He does not rank people by title or income level. He does not view people in terms of the power they wield. Since God does not view us this way, we should not view the people who work for us in that way.

Let's suppose you are a manager over a large plant. Someone makes a big mistake. You are about to rub that person's nose in the mistake when someone says, "Be careful, remember that person is the boss's daughter." Will that change your tone and the words you choose? Will you adopt the attitude of teacher rather than disciplinarian? Most likely you will. The point Paul is making is this: the people who work for us are the sons and daughters of God most High!

If you have authority over others, one of the biggest challenges is not "lording it over them." You have a job to do. However, one of your biggest jobs is to encourage and motivate those who work under you. The best way to do that is to show people that they have value in your eyes and that their contribution makes a difference.

Conclusion

I hope you have seen that Paul has been operating from a simple premise: a person who truly decides to follow Christ will relate to people differently than one who has not turned to Christ. Having been recipients of an undeserved grace, we will work to extend that grace to others. This is true whether it is a wife to her husband, a husband to his wife, a child to their parents, or a parent toward his child, an employee toward their employer or the way an employer treats those who work for them. Christianity that does not have a practical effect is not genuine Christianity.

I hope you have been attracted to the kind of relationships Paul talks about in our text. Let's examine how to enrich those relationships.

The way to a better relationship with those around you is to address your relationship with God. Instead of arguing that God "owes you" because you are such a decent person, you need to see that if God gave you what you truly deserve, you would spend eternity in Hell! Instead of arguing with God, begin by bowing before Him, asking for the mercy He offers us through Jesus. Our Lord paid the price for our rebellious and stubborn ways. We will not, and cannot, be right with God apart from what Jesus has done for us. We do not earn salvation, we receive it.

Once we become a recipient of grace; once we know that we have been delivered from death to life due to nothing we have done; we will be able to drop that sense of superiority that poisons relationships. We will discover what it means to be loved for who we are and not for what we have produced. Once we experience this love, we will be able to start seeing others as those in need of love. We will relate to each other with compassion rather than arrogance; with dignity rather than superiority; with grace rather than with power. And when that happens we will see other people change. And once people begin to change, we hopefully will also see that many of the things that really need to be changed in our world will change not because of our complaining, but by His grace.

Dig Deeper

1. How was slavery in the time of Paul different from the slavery we think of in the United States?
2. What does the way we work declare about what we believe?
3. Why is "doing your job" important for a Christ-follower?
4. What responsibilities does an employer have to their employees and why?
5. What options are available to a person who works for someone they don't like?

21
Knowing the Enemy
Ephesians 6:10-12

We want to be followers of Christ. But, I suspect your experience is like mine: it is a battle. I find myself with hundreds of excuses why I "can't" do what God has told me to do. My mind drifts to thoughts I do not welcome or desire. Even though I know God is in control, there are times when I am discouraged at the seeming lack of progress in my spiritual life. I sometimes wonder if I truly am a new creation in Christ.

I believe these were the same feelings we see in the apostle Paul. In Romans 7 he reflects on his struggle,

> *I want to do what is right, but I can't. I want to do what is good, but I don't. I don't want to do what is wrong, but I do it anyway. But if I do what I don't want to do, I am not really the one doing wrong; it is sin living in me that does it. I have discovered this principle of life—that when I want to do what is right, I inevitably do what is wrong. (Romans 7:18-21, NLT)*

I am glad Paul shared his experience with us because my experience matches his. The question is, why is following Christ so difficult? Paul answers that question in the text before us.

> *A final word: Be strong in the Lord and in his mighty power. Put on all of God's armor so that you will be able to stand firm against all strategies of the devil. For we are not fighting against flesh-and-blood enemies, but against evil rulers and authorities of the unseen world, against mighty powers in this dark world, and against evil spirits in the heavenly places. (Ephesians 6:10-12, NLT)*

We Are in a Supernatural Battle

There are three things to notice immediately. First, we are in a *supernatural* battle. It is something bigger than we can see and greater than we can overcome (in our own strength.).

Second, it is a *personal battle*. The word for "fighting" (v. 12) is sometimes translated "wrestle." The picture is of two people swaying back and forth while locked in battle. It is a hand to hand fight. This is not just some vague notion of the Devil and His army doing battle with God and His angels. The idea here is that we *personally* are involved in a battle with the Devil and his army. It is the difference between watching a boxing match and actually being in the ring as one of the boxers. This is personal.

Third, the fight cannot be won on our own. Paul doesn't tell us to "buck up." He tells us to be strong "in the Lord." Our only hope in this battle (with a much superior enemy) is to draw on the strength of the Lord. It is the difference between fighting a World War by yourself and fighting with the help of the Army, Navy, Air Force, and Marines!

The Nature of the Battle – The Enemy

Paul tells us that we are fighting

> *against evil rulers and authorities of the unseen world, against mighty powers in this dark world, and against evil spirits in the heavenly places (Ephesians 6:12, NLT)*

I find this difficult to grasp because I don't know how to relate to an unseen world. However, throughout the Bible, the reality of a spirit world is seen clearly. In the book of Genesis we see the Serpent in the Garden. Angels show up in Sodom. An Angel appeared to Daniel and talked about a fight with Satan's forces. Elisha was surrounded by angels. The Shepherds listened as the angels declared God's deliverance had come. Jesus was tempted by the Devil personally. Demons possessed people in New Testament days and were cast out by Jesus.

Many believe the Bible describes the Devil as a fallen angel. He rebelled against the authority of God (apparently long before the creation of mankind). Our conclusion is God must have given the angels the ability to rebel. Satan chose to rebel against God. He took with him a third of the angels of Heaven (who are now demons). Satan's goal is to turn us from the Lord or at least make us irrelevant in the battle (by encouraging a lukewarm or half-hearted faith).

There are many unanswered questions. The Bible is silent on details. Perhaps this is to keep us from getting overly fascinated with the Devil.

Satan continues to send temptation through random thoughts in our head (the brief thought that we could "run someone down in the road.") Discouragement, a sense of defeat, or on the other extreme: arrogance and self-righteousness, are tools of Satan. He attacks us at our point of weakness.

From the book of Job it appears Satan has power to cause bad things to happen. He can even afflict us with disease! This does not mean that every disease or bad thing is caused by Satan...it just means he can do these things. The difference between a test and a temptation is the way we respond to the things Satan sends our way.

There are three mistakes when it comes to Satan. The first mistake is to take Him lightly. Satan would like nothing better than for us to conclude he is not real. He encourages us to make caricatures of Him and to believe that there is "no rational reason to believe in a Devil." There is no opponent easier to defeat than the one who doesn't see you coming.

The second mistake is to become preoccupied with the Devil. We see him lurking around every corner until we become paralyzed with fear. Satan loves this extreme also. Since we see him everywhere, he has us preoccupied without ever having to do a thing! Satan is a powerful and skilled enemy. However, his power is limited by the Lord. He cannot "make" us sin. He is not all-powerful. He cannot be everywhere (most of us will never be tempted by the Devil himself but by his minions). He does not know everything (though he is much smarter than we are). Satan is already defeated by Christ...he just hasn't stopped fighting. One of the Psalmists writes,

For who in all of heaven can compare with the LORD;

What mightiest angel is anything like the LORD?

The highest angelic powers stand in awe of God.

He is far more awesome than all who surround his throne. (Psalm 89:6-7, NLT)

The third mistake is to use the reality of the Devil to excuse our sinful behavior. Satan will tempt us. He will encourage us to sin. He will fill our minds and thoughts with all manner of evil...but he does not make us sin. Sin is a choice we make! We are responsible. We can't hide behind the excuse that "we are weak" because God has made all His power available to us in the person of the Holy Spirit. If we do not take hold of that power...WE are the ones responsible.

The Strategies of the Enemy

Do you remember the movie "Groundhog Day"? In the movie Bill Murray has to re-live the same day (Groundhog Day) again and again. Eventually Murray used the repetition to learn about his Producer (Andie MacDowell). Each day Murray fixed the mistakes he made the day before. Apparently he re-lived the day for a long time because he learned how to do many things and got to know all the people of the town. He had time to perfect what he was doing by doing it over and over.

Satan has been tempting people for a very long time. He has perfected his craft of undermining believers. He knows our points of vulnerability and will exploit them at any opportunity. We need to understand the superior skill of our enemy.

Satan has many different approaches,

- He will attack God's character (as in the Garden of Eden).
- He will mix a little truth with a lot of error.
- He will misquote Scripture so that it says something it never meant to say.
- He will try to persuade us that good can be attained if we do what God has declared to be wrong. In other words he will try to convince us that God doesn't know what He is talking about.
- He will encourage us to trust our own efforts for attaining salvation.
- He will encourage us to pray to angels or even people who have died rather than truly talk to the Lord of All.

- He will try to get us ensnared by worldliness. In other words he encourages us to "love the world" so this love for the approval, trophies and values of the world squeezes out time for the Lord.
- He encourages pride so we feel we can stand in judgment over others or believe that our passions and gifts are more significant or important than others.

The late Welsh Pastor, D. Martyn Lloyd Jones wrote,

> *Pride manifests itself in many different ways. It makes us oversensitive; and when we are over-sensitive we are very easily hurt, and we feel hurt. What havoc has been wrought in the Christian church in this way! Pride, as manipulated by the devil, leads to jealousy, to envy, to a sense of grudge because we are not being appreciated, and someone else is being put before us. In this way the devil can upset a church or a community; and he has often done so. His object always is to spoil God's great handiwork, and especially the most glorious thing of all, the grace of God in salvation within the church!*[36]

He will endeavor to throw us out of balance. The Christian life is a balance between our mind, emotions, and behavior. It is like a three-legged stool. When in balance, it is very steady. However, if one leg is missing or longer or shorter than another, it is unbalanced and unsafe. The same is true in our spiritual lives. It is important to know what we believe, but if knowledge never translates into behavior, it is out of balance. We must not simply know the truth, we must believe it to the core of our being.

He will create division. Think of the people who have been harmed in their faith because of a division that took place in a church. Often it was a division over something very minor.

Satan will keep our focus on our experiences. Experience is important but if "having an experience" is all that we are about, we will be out of balance. Satan loves to have us judge worship, a study session, a quiet time of devotion, or even what is right and wrong by how we "feel" about something. When we become obsessed with our feelings we are out of balance.

He will get us to trust gimmicks, follow charismatic leaders, and be swayed by Christian peer pressure rather than trust the Lord and His Word. I think Satan encourages the idea of celebrity Pastors. He wants us to focus on people rather than the Lord. He wants us to compete with others to build "our Kingdom." He will try to get us to think our kingdom and God's kingdom are one and the same…they are not.

He will create false religions. Every religion has people who tell you how it has "changed their lives" (the overemphasis on experience at the expense of truth.) What characterizes a false religion? There are a few telltale signs,

- It is relatively new.
- It centers on a charismatic leader rather than on Christ. It is always wise to ask who the founder of this particular religion is.
- It appeals to a different authority than the Bible. Sometimes that authority is other texts (the Book of Mormon, the Koran, Science and Health (Christian Science), Dianetics (Scientology) etc.) That authority may also be human reason, contemporary "scholarship", or even "science." The point is, they will always sidestep the full authority of God's Word.
- It denies essential doctrines. One of the first doctrines to go is any teaching on sin. Sin does not appeal to people so it is eliminated. The unique deity of Christ, the literal resurrection, the death of Christ as a sacrifice for our sin, and Jesus as the only way to be right with God are often cast aside. The absence of any of these truths indicates it is a false religion.
- It will prescribe a way of salvation that involves following a formula rather than trusting Christ. Every other religion gives a prescription…only Christianity announces good news.

The point of all of this is to alert you to the need for constant readiness. Satan is resourceful. He knows that different temptations will be effective with different people. If we are not prepared he can shred us.

Winning the Battle

Paul gives us two pieces of advice: First, we are to be strong in the Lord. We are overmatched when it comes to battle with the Devil and his army. We cannot defeat him in our own strength. Our strength must be found in the Lord. The only way to walk in victory is to walk as close to the Lord of life as possible.

Second, Paul tells us to put on the full armor of God. God has given us the tools that we will need to stand our ground with the Devil. These tools are listed as: the belt of truth, the breastplate of righteousness, the shoes of peace, the shield of faith, the helmet of salvation, and the sword of the Spirit. Finally, our greatest resource is prayer.

In short, we are told to hold on to the truth about God's character and His grace and walk in the path that He tells us to walk. Think about a music teacher who is teaching a new song. She hands out music for the various parts. If the band is going to sound good they need to all play the music on the paper. If everyone "freelanced" you would not have music, you would have noise! If we want to become good musicians we need to trust the music. It is the same way here: the key to success and victory is to trust our commanding officer and follow His map. To do otherwise is to walk right into the trap of the enemy.

Conclusion

We should not be surprised living the Christian life is hard. We should not even be surprised by the thoughts which pop into our head or the discouragement, guilt, and condemnation that often comes upon us...Satan is at work! The only way to stand against such temptation is to cover ourselves, hide ourselves, and surround ourselves with the truth of God.

There is a sense in which the fierceness of the battle depends on whether or not we are perceived as a threat to Satan by the way we live and believe. He picks his targets carefully. I don't know about you, but I find that thought a little unnerving. It means if we are not facing temptation, the Devil does not see us as a threat!

I find that I often give in to temptation without a fight. The truth is, the more you resist, the more fierce the temptation will become. No one endured a temptation that was more fierce than Jesus. He resisted until he was victorious. Most of us give in because we are tired or don't want to fight. We will never gain victory unless we are ready for the battle.

Maybe it will help you to remember that if you are tempted, though the struggle to follow Him seems difficult, it is not necessarily a sign of weakness…it may be a sign that Satan and his army sees you as a threat. (In other words, something must be going right in your life).

We have witnessed some trying times. In response to the Gulf War in 1991 at the NHL all-star game in Chicago the fans broke into a stunning cheer during the National Anthem that filled every American with a sense of pride. When 9/11 took place Americans rallied behind President Bush as he stood defiantly upon the rubble and said, "I hear you…and soon the whole world will hear you." Right after the Boston bombing during the Boston Marathon at a Boston Bruins hockey game 20,000 people stood together and sang the National Anthem with one voice. It was a moving scene. We have been touched by the acts of heroism in times of crisis. These are amazing moments of people meeting adversity with strength and faith.

That resilience, that sense of fight, that same spirit of determination is how we must meet the times of temptation as disciples of Christ. We must run to the Lord, draw strength from each other, and determine that we will not give in to the terrorists seeking to destroy our faith. We must be prepared and determined to stand against the dark forces and mighty powers in the spiritual world. We are not alone! As we rely on His strength we can and will …know victory.

Paul has given us our instructions. It is now time to get to work and live out the magnificent salvation that is ours through the grace and mercy of our Lord Jesus Christ. It is time to walk with Jesus.

Dig Deeper

1. Have you ever had a time when you felt you were being stalked by Satan? Describe that experience. How did you get through the time of trial?
2. Do you have any experiences with supernatural beings?
3. What temptation or strategy does Satan use against you most effectively?
4. What are some examples of false teaching you have become aware of?
5. Why do you think we trust our ability and strength rather than trust His?
6. What do you think each piece of the armor represents practically?

Bruce and Rick Goettsche

[1]Tim Keller, (2012) *The Freedom of Self-forgetfulness* Introduction. 10 Publishing.

[2] Quoted in Tim Keller, (2012) *The Freedom of Self-forgetfulness* Chapter 2

[3] William Barclay, ed., (1976). The letters to the Galatians and Ephesians. *The Daily Study Bible Series* (140). Philadelphia, PA: The Westminster John Knox Press.

[4] D. Martyn Lloyd Jones, *Christian Unity* (78). Grand Rapids, MI: Baker Books.

[5]D. Martyn Lloyd-Jones, (1982). *Darkness and Light: An exposition of Ephesians 4:17-5:17*. Grand Rapids, MI: Baker Books.

[6] William Barclay, ed., (1976) The letters to the Galatians and Ephesians. *The Daily Study Bible Series* (155). Philadelphia, PA: The Westminster John Knox Press.

[7]G. C. Jones, (1986). *1000 illustrations for preaching and teaching* (286). Nashville, TN: Broadman Press.

[8] Brant Hansen, (2015). *Unoffendable* (5). Nashville, TN: W Publishing Group.

[9] Ibid. (12)

[10]M. P. Green, Ed., (1989). *Illustrations for Biblical Preaching: Over 1500 sermon illustrations arranged by topic and indexed exhaustively*. Grand Rapids, MI: Baker Book House.

[11]Frederick Buechner, (1973). *Wishful Thinking: A Theological ABC* (2). New York: Harper & Row.

[12] Les Carter, (2003). *The Anger Trap*. Grand Rapids, MI: Baker.

[13] R. Kent Hughes, (1990). *Ephesians: The mystery of the body of Christ. Preaching the Word* (152). Wheaton, IL: Crossway Books.

[14] M. D. Dunnam & L. J. Ogilvie, Eds., (1982). *Vol. 31: Galatians / Ephesians / Philippians / Colossians / Philemon. he Preacher's Commentary Series* (214). Nashville, TN: Thomas Nelson Inc.

[15]John Piper, "Make your mouth a means of grace" (October 12, 1986), http://www.desiringgod.org/resource-library/sermons/make-your-mouth-a-means-of-grace

[16] A. W. Tozer & R. Eggert, (1998). *vol. 2: The Tozer Topical Reader* (229). Camp Hill, PA: Wingspread.

[17] John Ortberg, (2003). *Everybody is Normal Till You Get to Know Them* (66). Grand Rapids, MI: Zondervan.

[18]Max Lucado, *Anxious for Nothing* Location 884 and Henri Nouwen, *The Essential Henri Nouwen* (132-32).

[19]D. Martyn Lloyd-Jones (1998). *Life in the Spirit* (15). Grand Rapids, MI: Baker Books.

[20] James Montgomery Boice, (1988). *Ephesians: An Expositional Commentary* (189). Grand Rapids, MI: Ministry Resources Library.

[21] Timothy J. Keller, (2013). *The Timothy Keller Sermon Archive.* New York City: Redeemer Presbyterian Church.

[22] Ibid.

[23] Gary Thomas, (2015). *A Lifelong Love* (247). Colorado Springs, CO: David C Cook.

[24] Charles Swindoll, (1993) *Flying Closer to the Flame* (85). Waco, TX: Word Publishing.

[25] Gary Thomas, (2016). *Cherish: The One Word that Changes Everything for Your Marriage* (locations 345 & 361). Carol Stream: Tyndale.

[26] Tim Savage, (2012). *No Ordinary Marriage* (77-90). Wheaton, IL: Crossway.

[27] Ibid., (83)

[28] John Chrysostom, "Homily XX on Ephesians," quoted in John Meyendorff, (1984) *Marriage: an Orthodox Perspective, 3rd rev.* ed. (89-90). Crestwood, NY: St. Vladimir's Seminary Press.

[29] B. B. Barton & P. W. Comfort, (1996). *Ephesians. Life Application Bible Commentary* (118). Wheaton, IL: Tyndale House Publishers.

[30] Timothy J. Keller, (2013). *The Timothy Keller Sermon Archive.*

[31] Francis and Lisa Chan, (2014) *You and Me Forever* (Location 1870 Kindle Edition). San Francisco, CA: Claire Love Publishing.

[32] Ibid.

[33] R. Kent Hughes, (1990). *Ephesians: The mystery of the body of Christ. Preaching the Word* (206). Wheaton, IL: Crossway Books.

[34] J. Vernon McGee, (1997). *Vol. 5: Thru the Bible Commentary* (electronic ed.) (276). Nashville: Thomas Nelson.

[35] Dennis E. Bakke, (2005). *Joy at Work* (75). Seattle, WA: PVG.

[36] D. Martyn Lloyd-Jones, (1976*). The Christian Warfare: An Exposition of Ephesians 6:10–13* (91–92). Edinburgh; Carlisle, PA: Banner of Truth Trust.

Other Books by Bruce and Rick Goettsche

Difficult People: Dealing with Those Who Drive You Crazy

Other Books by Bruce Goettsche

Faith Lessons: Lessons in Faith from Genesis
Lessons in the Wilderness (Exodus - Deuteronomy)
Songs of the Heart - Psalms that Connect
Joy: Finding it, Keeping it (Philippians)
Finding Your Way Through the Fog (Colossians)
A Christian Handbook for Surviving Divorce
Rebuilding Life After Grief and Loss
Meeting with God Year 1 (Devotional)
Meeting with God Year 2
Meeting with God Year 3

Contact the Authors

Bruce@unionchurch.com and Rick@unionchurch.com

www.unionchurch.com
YouTube Channel: UnionchurchLH

Made in the USA
Columbia, SC
26 March 2019